CW00544328

Land's End to John O'Groats

First leg of our walk: surfers on Fistral Beach, Newquay

Land's End to John O'Groats

WALKING THE LENGTH OF BRITAIN IN 7 STAGES

Helen Shaw & Bob Shelmerdine

First published in Great Britain by Merlin Unwin Books Ltd, 2017

Merlin Unwin Books Ltd
Palmers House, Corve Street
Ludlow, Shropshire SY8 1DB

www.merlinunwin.co.uk

ISBN 978-1-910723-39-5

Printed by Great Wall

Typeset in 12 point Minion Pro by Merlin Unwin Books

This book is dedicated to Helen's Mum, who encouraged us to go, and willed us to finish before she died, and who, at the end, was immensely proud of our achievement.

Edna Shaw 1920-2015

CONTENTS

WHY DID WE DO IT?

What's the point of doing the Land's End to John O'Groats walk? Well, I suppose, like Everest, because it's there. Also because we wanted to make a salute to our country and to honour its scenery, people, places and history.

It is an epic voyage. You only have to do it once and the achievement is with you for the rest of your life. Whenever you sit down, you sit down as someone who has walked 1,140 miles, but you bounce up out of the chair at the whisper of a stroll.

Mind you, we are doing it again. We've got the bug and don't want to stop. One of the hardest parts of the walk was getting close to the end and wondering what on earth we were going to do next. The solution was very simple and extremely satisfying. Start all over again but along a different route. Explore yet more of our amazing country. It has taken a hold on us and we don't mind at all.

Did we get fed up during the walk? The answer is a very definite NO! The hardships, blisters and tiredness are instantly forgotten. Some who have written about the walk complain of boredom, drudgery and horrendous weather beating them into submission. It was never like that for us. There wasn't a worst bit. It was all fascinating. To go through the seasons, to smell the earth warming up from the winter, and even in the bad weather to be outside in blustery air all day and to see the wind billowing over the meadows, wave after wave, was a complete and utter joy.

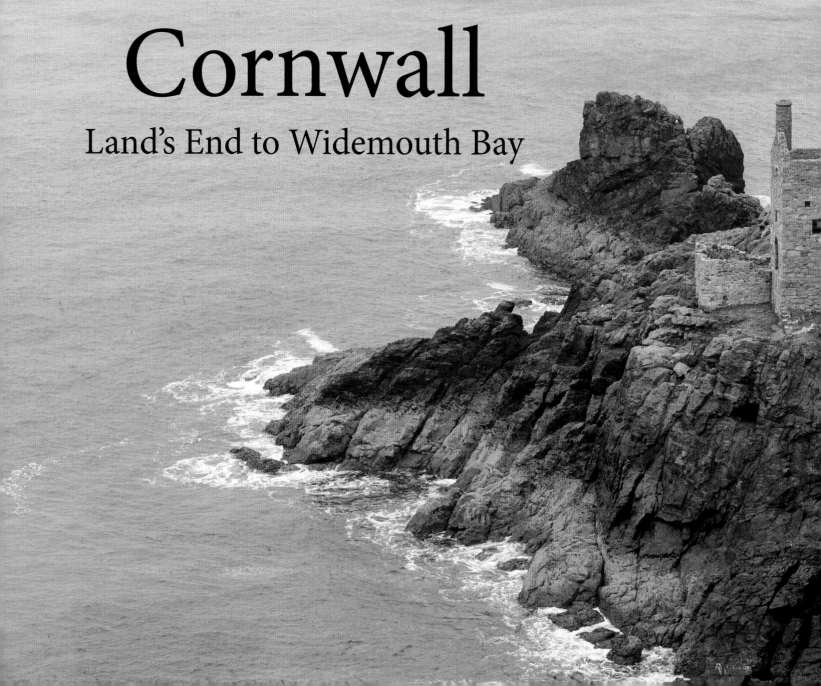

STAGE 1

10 Days – 119 miles

Cornwall

Land's End to Widemouth Bay

The Crowns Engine Houses, Botallack

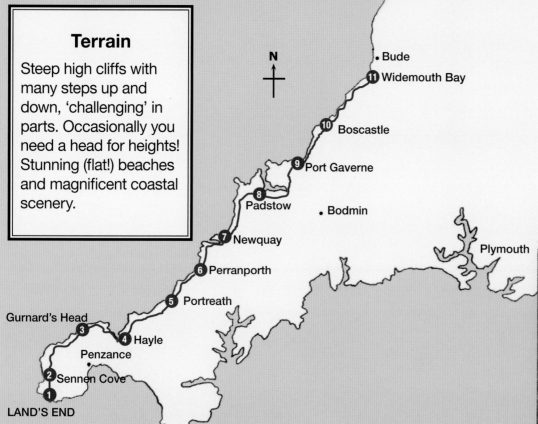

Terrain

Steep high cliffs with many steps up and down, 'challenging' in parts. Occasionally you need a head for heights! Stunning (flat!) beaches and magnificent coastal scenery.

DAY 1	Land's End to Sennen Cove	2 miles
DAY 2	Sennen Cove to Gurnard's Head	11.5 miles
DAY 3	Gurnard's Head to Hayle	13 miles
DAY 4	Hayle to Portreath	11 miles
DAY 5	Portreath to Perranporth	12 miles
DAY 6	Perranporth to Newquay	11.5 miles
DAY 7	Newquay to Padstow	17 miles
DAY 8	Padstow to Port Gaverne	11 miles
DAY 9	Port Gaverne to Boscastle	15 miles
DAY 10	Boscastle to Widemouth Bay	15 miles

DAYS 1 AND 2 – *Land's End to Gurnard's Head*

Standing under the sign at Land's End, you are about to start your great adventure. Ignore the tourist tat in the shops and the people who have driven there just to say that they have been to Land's End. Yours is the more noble purpose. You probably feel excitement and fear in equal measure. But turn your face north, take the first step, and you have begun.

Today's walk features Land's End itself with Longships Lighthouse in the distance and stunning coastal scenery, but otherwise this section is all about mines. Picturesque redundant red brick mine chimneys and engine houses litter the steep cliffs. At the gloriously-named Levant and Geevor mines, their history is brought to life. Five hundred people once worked here, men and boys and women (bal-maidens), dressing the ore brought to the surface, certainly since the Middle Ages, until the last such employee was made redundant in the early 1920s. In the 1850s there were at least 6,000 women employed in Cornish mines and many more in related industries in the area.

Set apart from the main mine are the arsenic works, inside which is displayed a grainy black and white image of some of the men who used to work there. Do their modern ancestors come in pilgrimage to stare at grandfathers and great-grandfathers who probably died young, poisoned by the only work available? In 1841 the average age of death in Redruth was 28 years and 4 months. Life had barely begun before it was over. Here the ground itself is still tainted, the grass a lurid lime green streaked with orange and purple.

Below: Longships Lighthouse off Land's End, at dawn

Geevor Mine Arsenic Works

In some places on the Land's End to John O'Groats walk we filled bottles from streams and dunked heads in cool pools, but not here. Apart from nefarious uses by Victorian poisoners (I've watched my share of black and white films!) arsenic had a great many uses, from controlling the Colorado beetle to use in pigments and dyes in the Lancashire cotton factories where my own Grandmother worked. I feel a connection to these long dead arsenic workers, knowing that what they endured was just part of a chain of working class misery. But arsenic has some interesting qualities.... it is found in a great many foods, most notably rice and cereal, but most arsenic has no smell or taste so there is no way to tell if your husband or wife is busily trying to poison you. Yikes.

DAY 3 – *Gurnard's Head to Hayle*

The sea is tropical blue, the sun is shining and today you are walking, strong and confident. Everything feels glorious. The Cornish coast is magnificent, living up to its reputation, with huge rollers roaring in and the wind tearing the spray back to make rainbows in the spume. There are seals in a sheltered cove, playing in the waves. In the distance, St Ives gleams like a jewel in a turquoise ocean. The town is justifiably famed for the quality of its light, for on the day we visited, it was sharp, intense, lustrous. Here is Tate St Ives, worth a visit if only to see the magnificent Patrick Heron window which reflects the brazen colours of the town. There are narrow, pretty little streets, glorious beaches, palm trees, and, unfortunately, hordes of visitors.

St Ives

DAY 4 – *Hayle to Portreath*

A day for grand landscapes, with a literary twist! One of the beauties of walking across your own country is that you begin to notice the detail. Today, on the long, clean Towans beach, look out for the amazing patterns in the sand created where waves have shifted grains around colourful pebbles. It's abstract art worthy of inclusion in the Tate and such a delight that it is the creation of nature, not man.

Off the coast, and guarding a dangerous reef, is Godrevy Lighthouse, the inspiration for Virginia Woolf's novel *To the Lighthouse* which was published in 1927. Apparently she spent hours looking out at the view from her balcony in St Ives, and who can blame her?

Ever present along the coast, all the way to Newquay, are the surfers, constant companions along this coastline.

One recommendation for sore feet – paddle in the sea. In March it is totally icy but my goodness, they feel amazingly brand new afterwards, and Portreath beach is a great spot to try it out!

Surfer, Towans Beach

Ralph's Cupboard, Portreath

DAY 5 – *Portreath to Perranporth*

Today follows a similar pattern of ups and downs in a bitterly cold gale, but the sun is still spring-bright and the sea delivers a special surprise: a pod of minke whales surface and arch their shiny black backs in graceful symmetry.

On top of the high cliffs lies an old airfield, Nancekuke, where sarin gas was produced by the MOD in the 1950s. The plant has been decommissioned many years ago and in theory any contamination buried in old mine shafts but I confess I wouldn't be too happy knowing that it was on my doorstep. Local people were not aware until about 30 years after the event about the sarin.

Cligga Head, Perranporth

Looking back to Perran Beach from Ligger Point

DAY 6
Perranporth to Newquay

RNLI Lifeguards seem to be on every beach. It looks a great way to spend a day; that is until someone needs rescuing from surf or rip tides. The beaches are amazing, spotless and with little or no seaweed or flotsam on them. No one seems to clean them so maybe they are just naturally beautiful. If you can, paddle in the water for the 2 mile length of Perran Beach, or if it's summer, have a proper swim; it's delightful.

The approach to Newquay on the South West Coast Path is particularly interesting. In summer there is a passenger ferry at the mouth of the estuary, or, tides and weather permitting, you can walk up the estuary to a tiny boardwalk bridge across the channel. However, the bridge can be swept away (it had been, when we were there), in which case you can wade through, or continue up the south side of the estuary to the top. The sand/mud can feel quite unsupportive and you will definitely sink in a little, so take care. If all else fails you can follow a higher path or even the road. All the routes are interesting for the water birds and flora you are likely to see on the estuary.

Newquay is quite a shock. After so many pretty villages, this is urban Cornwall at its most tawdry. But ignore the takeaways and pubs and walk across town to Fistral Beach. If the wind is blowing and the surf is up, pick your spot, and sit to watch the theatre as the young men and women of the town show off their prowess in the waves. It is quite a spectacle.

DAY 7 – *Newquay to Padstow*

If ever you think you may be tiring of aqua blue sea, green cliffs and golden beaches, something round the next corner will convince you otherwise. Today it is the magnificent Bedruthan Steps that take your breath away: huge rock stacks (in local folklore, created by a giant to cross the beach) punctuate the sand like immense commas. There is a steep route down to the beach to explore further if you have the time and inclination. At Mawgan Porth, just before you reach the steps, is the famous Bedruthan Hotel. My familyL used to holiday here, and I remember as a child dressing up as a little Japanese girl and winning a prize. I believe the entertainment is a little more sophisticated these days, though on several occasions through Cornwall we enjoyed the sight of children playing on the beaches, digging in the sand with buckets and spades as big as themselves, so perhaps not all innocent joy has been lost.

The coast here is as wild as any other part of the walk so far and was responsible for many wrecks before a lighthouse was built on Trevose Head, which can be bypassed if you are eager to get into Padstow.

Padstow truly is Rick Stein's town. He has two upmarket restaurants, a hotel, a café, a delicatessen, a seafood school, a patisserie, a fish and chip shop, and doubtless much more. If you want to eat in one of the restaurants you will need to book ahead and there was even a queue for his takeaway fish and chips, but it is worth it. Mine cost £18, but where else can you have grilled sole fillets fresh from the sea, chips and bread and butter, eaten sitting on the harbour wall of one of the prettiest villages in Cornwall?

The Trescore Islands at Porthcothan

Padstow harbour

DAY 8 – *Padstow to Port Gaverne*

The delightful little ferry from Padstow across the River Camel to Rock is a wonderful start to the day. If you insist on walking every step of the way to John O'Groats then you can always walk up and down the ferry deck, as Bob did! The alternative here would be a very long trek upriver to Wadebridge and along busy roads to get you back into Rock. Not recommended. Just enjoy crossing the water and keep an eye out for seals, herons, and anything else of interest that the ferryman may point out. The ferry runs virtually all day every day but it's always best to double check landing and departure points if there's a big spring tide or a howling gale.

The South West Coast Path ignores the little town of Rock but it may be worth a quick detour as it is reputedly the home to more millionaires than anywhere else in Cornwall and has one of the two Michelin-starred restaurants in Cornwall. Around the corner, close to the beach, is the tiny church of St Enodoc with a quirky 13th century crooked steeple. John Betjeman is buried there as he spent childhood holidays close by.

There's a beautiful little bay at Polzeath and when we were there some girls were exercising horses on the beach. The animals seemed to sense they were in for a treat as they started to gallop towards the sea as soon as their hooves hit the sand, and they then seemed very reluctant to come out of the waves, despite some urging.

One of the beauties of the fact that you are walking from Land's End to John O'Groats is that as long as you walk from your start to your end point each day, you can meander wherever you like. Today you can miss out the headland leading to Pentire Point and cut across fields and quiet roads to rejoin the coast at Carnweather Point and onwards to tiny Port Quinn. Next is Port Isaac, the TV-famed village which, whilst undoubtedly pretty, tends to be full of tourists. The hotels are expensive so you are better off walking a little further to beautiful Port Gaverne which has a warm and welcoming hotel with great rooms and good food.

St Enodoc's Church, Trebetherick, near Rock

Day 9 – *Port Gaverne to Boscastle*

Be warned, this is a tough day. The cliffs are high and steep, and, worst of all, crumbling. Two days before we walked down them, some steep steps at the edge of the cliff near Jacket's Point simply fell into the sea. Fortunately no one was on the path at the time. The day's walk goes something like this: steep up, steep down, stream, steep up, top of crumbling, windy, scary cliff with 100 yards flat, steep down… you get the picture. There are in theory seven of these ups and downs before you reach Trebarwith Strand and you'll feel every one! Yet it won't matter. If, like us, you are lucky, you will be seeing the Cornish Coast at its best. The light is clean and pure and dazzlingly bright, the sea a myriad of blues and greens, the cliffs a riot of violets, primroses and gorse, and above you, as a constant companion, the sweetest songs of the skylarks. There were moments in this day that I will never forget.

And just over the next cliff, the castle of Arthurian legend and mystery, Tintagel, awaits. On a bright sunny day with a lot of

Below: Cornish dry stone walls   *Right: Tintagel Castle*

tourists wandering around, it does lose some of its magic. This is one place that would probably be better seen in mists or storms. Nevertheless it is something to behold, perched on its cliffs with the sea beating into caves below. There is no doubt that a significant settlement existed here in the Dark Ages, for remains have been found that prove this, but of course there is no evidence that it was ever the birthplace of King Arthur.

There are plenty of places to stay in the village or you can push on with one last effort to Boscastle, which is quieter and very pretty, with cottages gathered round an Elizabethan harbour. You may, however, just be too tired to appreciate it until the following morning when you have rested your legs a little.

Below: Barras Nose, Tintagel
Right: Spring flowers in St Gennys Churchyard, Crackington Haven

DAY 10 – *Boscastle to Widemouth Bay*

There is yet more up and down today, and after yesterday's monumental efforts, your calves will probably be feeling it! There is a pretty little diversion down a quiet streamy valley into Crackington Haven if you take the small path off the coast near The Strangles, and if you are very, very lucky you may even see an otter thereabouts. (we didn't, sadly.) Crackington is a haven, a good place for a short stop before you tackle the enormous, black-cliffed climb out and up. Once you reach the top you are in a different world. Here there are no tourists or souvenir shops, for only those who have the determination (and the lungs) to get up here enjoy the quiet peace disturbed only by the skylarks and the faint distant murmuration of the sea.

Somehow above the cliffs we lost the path, which was tiresome, but it meant we stumbled on the beautiful wildlife churchyard of St Gennys. If you happen to be in the area in spring, make the detour just to see the primroses, violets, daffodils and daisies sitting prettily in the dappled sunshine of this most peaceful of places.

Steep and eroding steps down cliffs between Crackington Haven and Millook

Back on the coast you come to the scariest moment of the whole walk so far. From the top of an enormous cliff the steps down seem to simply disappear over the edge. For anyone with even the faintest vertigo, it is quite simply terrifying to head down a path so sheer that you feel as if gravity will pull you forward over the cliff. Breathe deeply, concentrate on the steps, not the drop, and DO NOT trip!

Just to put it into perspective, the walk meter we use shows that on this day we climbed 2,100 feet and descended much the same.

On a clear day you can see the island of Lundy out in the Bristol Channel, which gives a surge of encouragement as you realise you have in fact progressed a long way north from Land's End. It feels like an achievement, although months later when you look back and review your pride at this moment, you will probably laugh because, actually, you still have a very long way to go!

At the end of this long day, Widemouth Bay appears. If you are following our route and are turning north-east into Devon from here, take this last opportunity to paddle in the sea and ease those sore feet, for you will not reach sea worth paddling in again until Dornoch, some 700 miles further north. There will be plenty of lovely lakes and streams though.

On reflection

There were days when, I confess, I cried. Sore feet and sheer weariness when faced with another 300 foot steep climb up steps tends to do that to me. I began to hate steps.

Yet my main feelings were not of pain or discouragement, they were of joy, freedom, pride, exhilaration, peace, wonder and interest. I felt a massive sense of achievement at the 100+ miles under our belts and on reaching a new county, Devon. I felt set apart from the rest of mankind; as if the coast of Cornwall was now mine, not conquered but lived and known and loved.

I leave Cornwall with lasting memories and a sense of great anticipation for what is to come. Next leg of the journey, we are going to Devon, over Exmoor, crossing the Quantocks and dropping down to the Somerset Levels, climbing the Mendips and walking into one of our favourite cities, Bristol. I can't wait.

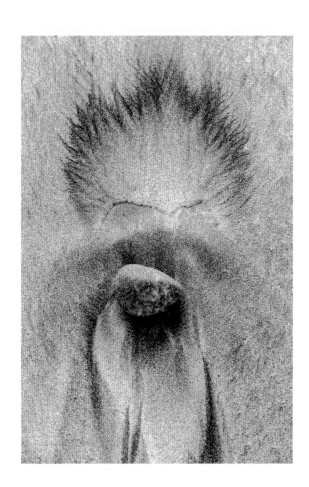

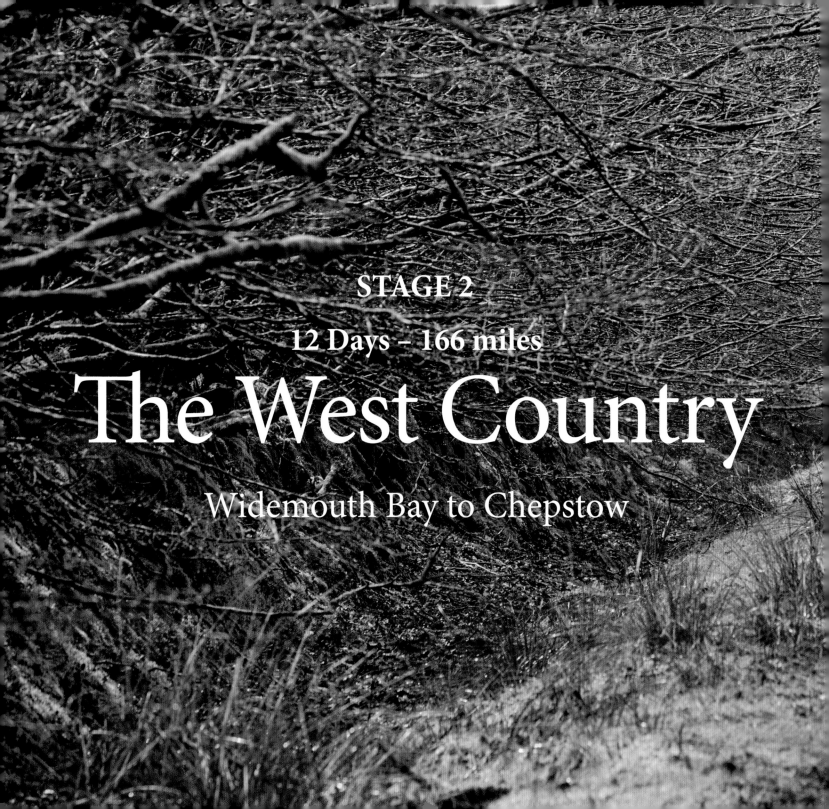

STAGE 2

12 Days – 166 miles

The West Country

Widemouth Bay to Chepstow

Exmoor, south of Withypool

Terrain

Very varied terrain on this section, ranging from the glorious rolling hills of Devon (still steep!) through to wild moorlands on Exmoor, up and down the precipitous escarpments of the Quantock Hills, across the flat and rather wet Somerset Levels, through the limestone gorges of Cheddar.

And finally over the Mendips, into Bristol and thence along the Severn Estuary to cross into Wales.

DAY 11	Widemouth Bay to Bradworthy		**DAY 17**	Radlet to Wedmore
	15 miles			24 miles
DAY 12	Bradworthy to Great Torrington		**DAY 18**	Wedmore to Draycott
	15 miles			5 miles
DAY 13	Great Torrington to South Molton		**DAY 19**	Draycott to Rickford
	17 miles			9 miles
DAY 14	South Molton to Withypool		**DAY 20**	Rickford to Bristol
	13 miles			14 miles
DAY 15	Withypool to Roadwater		**DAY 21**	Bristol to Henbury
	16 miles			8 miles
DAY 16	Roadwater to Radlet		**DAY 22**	Henbury to Chepstow
	17 miles + 3 to the pub & back!			13 miles

DAY 11 – *Widemouth Bay to Bradworthy*

There were mixed feelings today, for we turned our backs on the coast and the blue sea that had been our constant companion for ten days, knowing that we would not walk by the ocean again until the north of Scotland. If your route is the same as ours though, you may also heave a sigh of relief that there are no more coastal cliffs to climb. I know I did.

There were other contrasts today. Mostly the walking is on quiet country lanes which is pleasant but rather hard on the feet so it was during these few days that I developed the first real blisters that would then plague me all the way to Glasgow. Very often the first job on arrival in the evening (and sometimes even during the day too) was to do a little surgery on my blisters with a needle. It worked, usually, but it hurt. A lot.

If you are walking in spring, as we did, the high banks of the Devon lanes are covered in primroses, violets, celandines and many other spring delights. A slight detour of several hundred yards up to the lovely café at Lower Tamar Lakes was worth it. Bradworthy was full to bursting with a tractor rally when we arrived but you are advised to book ahead if you are planning to stay here as it's only a small village.

We decided not to eat out but to eat in our room. We ended up with tinned potatoes, tinned sweetcorn and tough roast beef, all cold. It was one of the low points of the whole journey.

DAY 12 – *Bradworthy to Great Torrington*

Blisters and shin splints today. We hadn't had a rest since the start and two days of pounding on roads led to pressure blisters on my heel and with Bob developing shin splints. Both limping, we re-named our destination Great Totterington!

It was yet more quiet lanes today but we adopted a slightly southerly route from Bradworthy and joined the delightful Tarka Trail which is on a disused railway. We loved it. It's flat, in the valley, with banks of wild daffodils and wood anemones, and some interesting sculptures. A most pleasant approach to the town, which lies on top of a steep hill. The lady at our accommodation (Higher Darracott Farm, about 2 miles outside town) had upgraded us to a self-catering cottage for the night and it was so perfect that we decided on the spur of the moment to take a rest day and stay for two nights.

On the second day we strolled into the town, luxuriating in the lack of weight on our backs, then on our return snoozed, wrote postcards, sat and listened to the comforting, homely sounds of the chickens clucking in the yard. If you feel ready for a break at this point, we can highly recommend it. Perfect peace and comfort!

Right: Exmoor ponies

Left: A rather wooden conversation with Bob, on the Tarka Trail outside Great Torrington

DAY 13 – *Great Torrington to South Molton*

The rest most definitely did us good and if you have done the same you may well be feeling full of bounce again today!

You may need it, as again the route onwards was mainly on quiet roads with not much interest except the primroses, though crossing the Taw at Umberleigh we did see a cormorant, sure sign that the water was clean and full of fish!

Woods full of primroses, deer and bluebells followed and were a sylvan break from the roads but unfortunately the final few miles into South Molton were on a busy 'B' road with no footpath. Watch out! We discovered that Devon drivers are quite mad.

South Molton, like Great Torrington, was a traditional, old fashioned town which seemed not to have joined the 21st century, but nevertheless had a quaint charm. At our town centre hotel we encountered timeless and, to be honest, rather boring locals playing bridge and chess in the bar, all of whom stared down their noses at us in a somewhat snooty manner. Perhaps, despite washing clothes every night, we could have been beginning to smell a little interesting by then.

Higher Darracott Farm, Great Torrington

Writing my diary before the detail of the day fades

DAY 14
South Molton to Withypool

Much excitement today as Exmoor was on the agenda and there was the chance to get off the roads and back onto tracks and paths: lovely!

The steep climb out of the valley towards the moor tested our legs but the views behind us across the rolling fields were very pretty. Almost as soon as we reached the moor we came across Exmoor ponies, which are small, stocky, fluffy and totally gorgeous. We also saw large herds of red deer in the distance. Exmoor has some famous hunts and evidence of their presence in horses and stables is everywhere, whilst all the pubs seem to be decorated with stuffed animals and antlers and frequented by the hunters themselves.

We admired the beautiful raised beech hedges growing on top of earth banks, for which the area is well known. Only in the West Country can you see these unique and ancient boundaries.

Withypool is a tiny, pretty village with a picturesque bridge over a sparkling river, and a pub where the food was excellent but the service very slow, so slow that a child on a neighbouring table complained very loudly 'Where's my pudding?' We decided not to risk the wait.

The River Barle at Withypool

DAY 15 – *Withypool to Roadwater*

Still on Exmoor today, we had more fine views as we climbed to over 1400 feet at one point and had the exciting sighting of the Bristol Channel and the coast of south Wales in the far distance. Of course there were miles to go before we reached either Bristol or Wales but the glimpse meant we would soon put Devon and Cornwall behind us. We walked part of the Coleridge Way, in the footsteps of poet Samuel Taylor Coleridge, known for his wanderings on Exmoor and the Quantocks.

The Way crosses the quiet and little-known Brendon Hills on the edge of Exmoor, to Roadwater. Unfortunately today was the one occasion on the whole walk when we came across a deliberately blocked public footpath. We decided to press on and skirted the blockage by a fairly exciting climb over a fence and into a steep and pathless wood. But at least we didn't retrace our steps (we hated doing that!) and emerged on the other side slightly scratched but satisfied. Our reward on the way to our B&B was seeing a magnificent dog fox, his coat russet red in the sunshine, crossing a nearby field. One the Exmoor hunters had missed!

Forest track outside Roadwater

DAY 16 – *Roadwater to Radlet*

We missed the best of the Quantocks, since it rained solidly all day.

The delightfully named Monksilver village is quintessentially English, with even a garden decorated with porcelain figures playing cricket and the church as backdrop *(below left)*. It could not have been any other country.

Before the climb up to the hills, do stop at the tiny station near Stogumber, on the West Somerset Heritage Railway which runs between Minehead and Bishops Lydeard. Even if there are no trains to see, the station is a delight and as for the waiting room….paradise! A brightly burning log fire, a tiny café with yummy cakes, and a friendly stationmaster called Tom. We divested all our wet gear and got warm by the fire, and dear Tom very kindly allowed us to eat our sandwiches inside too, even though we hadn't bought them from him. The climb up to the top of the Quantocks from Crowcombe is a steep one but I imagine on a fine day would be very pleasant. We just dripped, rustled and panted our way to the top, got lost on the way down, but arrived at a fabulous B&B with tea and cake on arrival and a double bed each!

DAY 17 – *Radlet to Wedmore*

It will be a very long day today if you decide to walk all the way into Wedmore. Be warned! The compensation is that it is mostly very flat, and never boring, since these are the Somerset Levels, so expect big skies and that kind of lucent quality to the air that expanses of water can create. Try not to get lost though as you may well find your way blocked by any number of deep or wide drainage channels. This happened to us and ended with a muddy scramble across a ditch, followed by some tears.

First however, you come to Bridgewater, something of a disappointment as I expected a pretty little historic town and it is instead a bit industrial and rather weary.

The King's Sedgemoor Drain is wide and graced with many swans, and in the distance the mysterious Tor at Glastonbury rises out of the Levels. You could take a more easterly route to visit the town itself and from there the beautiful cathedral city of Wells, but we carried on north heading resolutely for Bristol.

At the end of 24 miles, Wedmore was a welcome sight, though I was too exhausted to appreciate it. This was one day when I was completely, utterly, weary. Too tired to eat, I managed a little soup and was done.

DAY 18
Wedmore to Draycott

Since we were doing the walk in stages rather than as one long enterprise, we concluded our first stage at Wedmore and returned there some three weeks later on a fine early summer day to continue our journey.

We ended our crossing of the Somerset Levels with a short stroll to Draycott on the edge of the Mendips. Most of the village is given over to the growing of strawberries in huge polytunnels, and so famous is it for this that the now-disused railway is called the Strawberry Line. Nowadays the process is so sophisticated that feeding and watering the strawberry plants can even be controlled from a mobile phone. Apparently the village is also famous for its cider, though we saw no evidence of it.

Left: Tom, the station master at Stogumber

Right: The Somerset Levels outside Wedmore, looking towards Glastonbury Tor

Day 19 – *Draycott to Rickford*

Easing ourselves back into the walk, today was a gentle 9 miles.

Along the way we met another of those wonderful characters who pepper the Land's End to John O'Groats walk and whom we will always remember. This was a weathered man riding his quadbike on the quiet lanes who told us that he had wanted to be a farmer ever since he was five years old but instead had become a builder and only in his latter years had he achieved his ambition to own a smallholding.

The change to limestone Downs as we approached Cheddar brought a new landscape. The short grass turf and the limestone banks were hazily purple with violets, wild thyme, and orchids, interspersed with delicate cowslips nodding in the breeze. In the turf we noticed tiny holes at regular intervals and came to the conclusion they were the homes of little bees that popped in and out with industrious buzzing.

We chose not to walk through Cheddar Gorge itself as the road is narrow and busy but you can walk along the edge, high up on the cliff, and then drop down to cross the top of the gorge road where you can see the magnificent cliffs, and, later on at Burrington Combe, the rock that supposedly inspired the hymn *Rock of Ages*.

Here there were herds of goats grazing precariously on the cliff ledges – they were introduced to encourage the biodiversity of the area by keeping the vegetation short.

Left: Feral goats, Cheddar Gorge   *Above: the footpath plunges between the steep sides of Cheddar Gorge*

Colourful houses in the Hotwells district of Bristol

Clifton Suspension Bridge, Bristol

DAY 20 – *Rickford to Bristol*

Don't expect to have a beautiful walk by the shores of Blagdon Lake this morning, as the path alongside the lake is strictly restricted to fishermen. It means walking instead through fields. With very lively cows.

From this point onwards we followed the Monarch's Way right into Bristol. This path is supposedly the escape route taken by Charles II after his defeat by Cromwell at the battle of Worcester in 1651.

The route climbed through sunlit fields where the wind was sweeping across the long grasses in undulating waves. The closest you can get to seeing the wind, Bob said.

At the summit, Dundry Beacon, the vista opens up to the great city of Bristol in the distance below. Close above our heads the large jets bound for Bristol Airport roared down the flight path at regular intervals: quite a contrast between the nature you are immersed in and the technology of the modern world, which for most of the time on this walk you forget about. Bristol was our first city or even town of any size since Land's End and the cars, the noise and the people, all came as a shock!

DAY 21 – *Bristol to Henbury*

Bristol is one of the finest cities in Britain, and should be given a day to appreciate it. You can, like us, combine your exploration with progressing the walk west, but there are some things you should not miss in this fabulous place. Start in the harbours where Brunel's magnificent *SS Great Britain* can be visited and all the quays, warehouses and docks have been transformed into a vibrant area of bars and restaurants.

Converted warehouses, Bristol harbour

In the centre the buildings are an eclectic mix of Georgian, Victorian, and 20th century. For a fine vista of Bristol walk up Brandon Hill towards Cabot Tower (commemorating the 400th anniversary of the sailing from Bristol of John Cabot to what became Canada, and onwards towards stunning Clifton.

Here the atmosphere and the architecture changes, with peaceful and elegant Georgian and Regency squares, high-end shops and cafés, and, of course, the iconic Clifton Suspension Bridge, spanning the equally amazing Avon Gorge. If you see nothing else, see this. It is very high! Sadly it needs to be plastered with notices from the Samaritans offering help to those considering a leap from the top. The thought of it is terrifying and simply looking over the side turned my stomach quite queasy.

Finally we escaped from the hubbub of the city up on the Downs. On a sunny day the wide expanses of grassy Downs were a delight. We sat for a while to watch the human play going on around us before we finished the day by walking out west through quiet green woods in Coombe Dingle towards Blaise Castle parkland and Henbury, setting us well on the way for the following day's walk.

DAY 22 – *Henbury to Chepstow*

Today we rejoined the coast, if such the Severn Estuary can be called. It didn't tempt us to paddle, though shelducks and other waders seemed perfectly happy dabbling in the mud. Across the busy M5 and the new M49 we plodded through a fairly industrial area, which made a change, until the new and old Severn Crossings came into view ahead.

Both bridges are magnificent marvels of modern engineering, as spectacular as Brunel's Clifton masterpiece of the day before. On a hot day they seem to float insubstantially above the water. The new

The new Severn Bridge, seen from the old one

49

Above and opposite: Chepstow Castle

bridge is not open to pedestrians so you have to walk several miles further up by the side of the estuary to the old bridge to cross into Wales, and you have reached your second country on your epic walk!

It was quite an experience, crossing on the bridge. It is very high, with gaps in the walkway helping to emphasise the long drop to the muddy water beneath, and if you stop walking you will feel the unmistakable vibration and sway of the whole structure. I am sure it was safe, though it didn't feel like it!

On reflection

I wrote in my notebook about our day in Bristol: 'Today has been utterly joyous, I feel so close and so in love with Bob that my heart hurts. A wonderful, wonderful, day'. I think that after 23 days of being in each other's company for 24 hours a day, to be able to feel so happy says a great deal about our relationship!

By the time we reached Chepstow we had walked almost 300 miles. There was no longer any doubt in my mind that this was something we could do. I knew, by then, that nothing short of disaster would stop us. We had had days of joy, some of pain, but never boredom. Every turning, every path, field, street, person, was new and interesting. We were walking our land and loving it. And with so much still to come.

Ross-on-Wye

STAGE 3
13 Days – 181 miles
The Welsh Marches
Chepstow to Chester

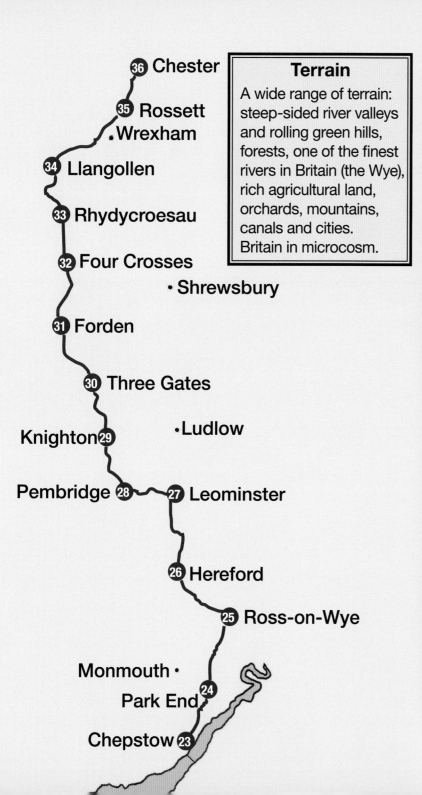

36 Chester
35 Rossett
· Wrexham
34 Llangollen
33 Rhydycroesau
32 Four Crosses
· Shrewsbury
31 Forden
30 Three Gates
Knighton **29**
· Ludlow
Pembridge **28** **27** Leominster
26 Hereford
25 Ross-on-Wye
Monmouth ·
Park End **24**
Chepstow **23**

Terrain

A wide range of terrain: steep-sided river valleys and rolling green hills, forests, one of the finest rivers in Britain (the Wye), rich agricultural land, orchards, mountains, canals and cities. Britain in microcosm.

DAY 23	Chepstow to Parkend
	12 miles
DAY 24	Parkend to Ross-on-Wye
	14 miles
DAY 25	Ross-on-Wye to Hereford
	15 miles
DAY 26	Hereford to Leominster
	13 miles
DAY 27	Leominster to Pembridge
	14 miles
DAY 28	Pembridge to Knighton
	15 miles
DAY 29	Knighton to Three Gates
	11 miles
DAY 30	Three Gates to Forden
	12 miles
DAY 31	Forden to Four Crosses
	16 miles
DAY 32	Four Crosses to Rhydycroesau
	13 miles
DAY 33	Rhydycroesau to Llangollen
	14 miles
DAY 34	Llangollen to Rossett
	19 miles
DAY 35	Rossett to Chester
	13 miles

Day 23 – *Chepstow to Parkend*

Chepstow Castle stands proud above the final mile of the River Wye and is worth a visit before you press on northwards. Construction started from 1067, less than a year after William the Conqueror was crowned king, which is impressive enough, but the history of this place goes even further back, since there are bricks in the castle which came from an earlier Roman Fort. A strategic place. The castle has the oldest wooden doors in Europe, at 800 years old, which are worth seeing in their own right.

At Chepstow you have a decision regarding your route. Having walked the southern part of Offa's Dyke path before, we chose instead to take a more north-easterly route up into the Forest of Dean, an unexplored area for us. However the walk up the Wye Valley from Chepstow to Monmouth if you follow the Offa's Dyke route is stunning.

Our way took us through woods heady with the scent of bluebells and ramsons, underneath a newly opened canopy of translucent beech. I identified, correctly and with much pride, a yellow pimpernel amongst the flowers too!

Above: Looking back to the river Severn

Bluebells, paths and bridges in Forest of Dean

DAY 24
Parkend to Ross-on-Wye

Huge, straight oak trees, long forest vistas, glade after glade carpeted with bluebells, straight flat ex-railway tracks to walk on, the Forest of Dean was heaven! It is one of the surviving ancient woodlands of Britain, being first an area for royal hunting, and although it seems incredible now it does also have an industrial past, being used for charcoal burning, coal mining, and iron working (hence the railways). Now all is peace. Deer graze in the quiet dells and if you are lucky (we weren't) you may see wild boar, of which evidence was everywhere in rooted piles of earth.

Once out of the forest we dropped steeply down to rejoin the Wye Valley Walk at Lydbrook, then climbed some 600 feet up again to an iron age hill fort from where a magnificent view opened up of Ross-on-Wye below us and the blue hazed Hay Bluff and Brecon Beacons off in the distance.

Ross was one of our most favourite places on the whole walk. It wasn't just the hotel (the King's Head) which was superb in every sense from bedroom to food to service, but the whole town appeared to have adopted the same attitude. Everyone we met was helpful and friendly, the town was pretty, historic and interesting, and the view down to the River Wye beautiful. You may have gathered, we liked Ross.

DAY 25 – *Ross-on-Wye to Hereford*

We used the Wye Valley Walk all the way into Hereford, and delightful it was too. Not always close companion to the river itself but meeting it often enough to satisfy, this day was a stroll through a rural idyll. Swans glided serenely past on the quietly whispering river, fields were dressed in orchids, the slopes leading down to the river steep and wooded. Orchards flaunted pink-tinged apple blossom and houses we passed were draped in wisteria. It felt as if there was no finer or more perfect corner of England and I for one will never forget the peace and

Left: Ross-on-Wye   *Below: Apple orchards near Hereford*

the joy I experienced walking through this landscape on a late spring day with the sun hot on my back and my beloved Bob beside me.

Beware however the longhorn cows you may come across in some fields! It was not a happy moment when they lowered their heads and appeared to be threatening to charge.

I had heard somewhere that Hereford had been ruined by modern development and whilst this may be true in some parts, the Cathedral area remains quite stunning. I desperately wanted to see the 13th century Mappa Mundi, which is displayed in the Cathedral, but sadly we were too late to go in.

What a marvellous building though. I find it quite incredible that these medieval cathedrals and castles were constructed without any machinery. What immense skill and dedication it took and how lucky we are in this country to still be able to wonder at them.

Deer tracks across a field near Ivington, south of Leominster

DAY 26 – *Hereford to Leominster*

We were so lucky on our walk with the most beautiful weather throughout bar just a few days' rain. Today was another stunner with clear blue sky and a very hot sun, almost too hot for walking! Much of the landscape, when looking at a vista from a rise, reminded us of Tuscany with rolling hills, lines of poplars, and occasional rape fields dotted gold.

Many of the orchards hereabouts are very large and clearly commercial operations but that didn't prevent them from being pretty with lines of blossom shimmering in the haze. Yes, it was that hot!

Some of the paths were quite overgrown with nettles which meant one of two choices – get badly stung or put full length trousers back on and boil. I did both and in consequence had rather hot and scratched legs by the end of the day.

Leominster was closed. Totally. It's a very pretty little town but amenities were few and far between! However the small B road into the town was very busy even at 9pm. Where were all the people going? Perhaps the centre of Leominster is a British Bermuda Triangle.

DAY 27 – *Leominster to Pembridge*

Our B&B owner last night had a reputation on the dreaded Trip Advisor for rudeness, which to be fair we didn't experience until breakfast when Bob asked for a fried egg and the gentleman simply said: "No. Read the menu. Scrambled or poached". Well!! Question – why run a B&B for over 15 years if you really dislike people?

We turned sharply left at Leominster, heading west back towards Presteigne where our plan was to rejoin the Offa's Dyke path and walk the northern part of it to beyond Llangollen, but it did seem a shame to miss out on the lovely old town of Ludlow, just to the north of Leominster. Still, what we discovered very quickly when planning and then walking this route, was that it is impossible to visit everywhere that you are interested in. To do so would be a lifetime's work.

We did get very lost for about an hour at the end of the day, trying to find our B&B on a farm. It was raining too and retracing our steps through muddy woods and along an old railway line put us both in a bad mood for a while. It happens. Be prepared to be a little grumpy now and then.

DAY 28 – *Pembridge to Knighton*

Our B&B owners at Pembridge were the total opposite of our Leominster experience. In Pembridge, the lady of the house talked 19 to the dozen! She was an interesting person though, frequently

Looking to Panpunton Hill from Knighton

62

travelling to Japan to lecture on running a B&B as part of farm diversification. We never really discovered why Japan in particular. Her husband told us that, as a child, he used to visit the legless cobbler in Pembridge who shuffled about on his bottom. It clearly had made a big impression on him.

It rained all day. Bob had a terrible cold too but insisted that he was OK to walk. We did have what was for us a luxurious coffee stop in Presteigne where we sat on damp benches under the shelter of the closed and deserted cricket pavilion and watched the rain pouring off the roof. Most of our coffee stops were much less comfortable, often cobbled up by sitting on a pile of logs or stones, or a grassy bank. It sounds alright, doesn't it? But when you really want a break and a good sit down there is nothing finer than a bench. The trouble was, we hardly ever found one in the right place at the right time. We can still remember some occasions when we found a good bench spot, and still comment, even if we are in the car, if we pass a suitably placed and shady bench.

At a tiny place called Dolley Green we finally stopped walking west and turned north again, back on the actual Offa's Dyke itself, and then we climbed. Up and up, our first big hills since the Quantocks, with a superb view into Wales from the top, which unfortunately was very windy, wet and cold.

Dropping sharply into Knighton you will walk through the golf course where you are likely to see as many sheep as golfers!

Left: Willow herb on a misty morning on Panpunton Hill
Below: Near Three Gates looking towards Offa's Dyke

Day 29 – *Knighton to Three Gates*

We thought that Knighton had been evacuated on the morning we left. 9am, Monday morning, no cars, no people, nothing. No rat race there!

Panpunton Hill is a very stiff pull up from Knighton, do not underestimate it! There is a strategically placed bench about two thirds of the way up which is worth sitting on not just to regain breath but for the view, which becomes increasingly beautiful as you climb. The landscape is rolling, steep, immensely pretty and historic, as you are on or next to Offa's Dyke for much of the day.

Stop a moment to stand on this magnificent structure. There are some 80 miles of the actual 1200 year old Dyke still in existence, making it Britain's longest ancient monument, and one of the most impressive ancient

Montgomery

earthworks in Europe. Imagine building all those miles of banking and ditches across wild exposed country, without a mechanized digger in sight. How many people did it take? How many years to complete it? It is astounding. And still no one can be certain what its purpose was. Did Offa, King of Mercia, mean it as a defence to keep out the Welsh? Or was it simply a boundary marker? If so, an impressive one! It has even been suggested that the Dyke may have been built on top of an earlier Roman wall, or a prehistoric track, but little archaeological evidence exists to support those theories.

Whatever it was, it sits now in the landscape as a monument to one man's determination and power, and provides us with a tiny glimpse into a darker past. It rolls across the hills, keeping its secrets, and as you tread on it you breathe in the history and imagine the people who once walked here before you.

Our B&B (New House Farm) was hidden away in the folds of the hills and was perfect. After a scorching hot day where we actively tried to walk in the shade, our room was huge, shady and cool, fragrant with beeswax on old wooden dressers, surrounded by pretty gardens where swallows darted across the lawn. The owner made us the best omelette I have ever tasted followed by strawberries for pudding and afterwards we strolled round the stunning garden in the soft warmth of a British summer evening. Total perfection.

DAY 30 – *Three Gates to Forden*

A climb up to the 1000 foot Kerry Ridgeway, another ancient trackway, rewarded us with extensive views down to the Montgomery Plain whilst the hazy mountains of mid Wales to the west shimmered in the heat. Along field edges

Shropshire Union Canal near Forden

Looking west to Powis Castle and the Cambrian Mountains, from Beacon Ring Hill Fort

without shade the heat was extreme, so much so that finally, in desperation, we found a big oak tree and sat beneath it whilst our shirts were laid out on the barley stalks of the field to dry. The crops dipped and swayed in the faint breeze and in the distance the 13th century Montgomery Castle dominated the plain from its hilly vantage point.

Because we wanted to stay in Montgomery itself but the mileage was too little from our start point, we walked past the town and then caught a bus back in to our accommodation. There were a number of times we did this on the walk since sometimes accommodation was hard to find in exactly the right place. However we were always scrupulous in ensuring that we walked every step, even walking back a few yards if a bus stopped too far ahead!

Montgomery itself is a great place to stop over. The town is really attractive, with a Georgian Town Hall and other quaint buildings around the square. Walk up to the castle and have a wander; it is another magnificent piece of our history that you will come across on this walk.

The meal that evening in a Michelin starred restaurant with rooms (the Checkers) counts as, not surprisingly, potentially the best of the whole trip. The only drawback with the hotel being that our room had such a low entrance to the bathroom that we both ended up with badly banged heads and dizziness!

DAY 31 – *Forden to Four Crosses*

Over the past few days you will have criss-crossed the border between England and Wales so many times that you will be totally confused as to which country you are in at any one time, and the theme continues for the next few days too. Even though many of the place names are undoubtedly Welsh, very often they are in Shropshire, indicating the changeable nature of this border over the centuries. Today, however, was an entirely Welsh day, starting with a cool walk through the trees of the Leighton Estate, infamously guilty of the creation of the horrible and ubiquitous Leylandii trees when one of their gardeners cross bred two types of cypress!

You could choose to take a lower path but if you are feeling fit and the weather is clear climb instead up to the top of Beacon Ring, a Bronze Age Hill Fort. There are lovely picnic benches on the top (yes, these are some of the benches we remembered!) where you can relax for a time and enjoy the incredible views into Wales towards Cader Idris and Plynlimon in the far west.

Then it was down steeply to the flood plain of the Severn where we joined the Shropshire Union Canal all the way into Four Crosses. We found it to be very pretty with good views across the plain to the Breidden Hills and it was a pleasant change to be walking on the flat for a few miles!

Day 32 – *Four Crosses to Rhydycroesau*

It was another scorchingly hot day for us, with the sun beating down on us from the limestone cliffs of Llanymynech Hill, ablaze with flowers and hundreds of butterflies. Mostly however the route was pleasant but unspectacular.

We got so hot that we had to stop and ask a man in his garden if he would fill our water bottles. He did, with ice cold filtered water! He had a Rolls-Royce and a Jag in his drive which he told us proudly was his hobby.

Your route after Trefonen depends where you have decided to stay. We had booked a hotel in Rhydycroesau itself but thought that it was to the east of the village so managed to get ourselves thoroughly lost in a wood, where we had to retrace our steps, then discovered that the only way out without going back for miles was through a private farmyard. We very naughtily tried to sneak through but the owner had very large savage dogs (fortunately tied up) which barked like the hounds of hell and consequently summoned a horde of tiny snappy dogs and the angry farmer's wife. There was nothing left to do but grovel apologetically and beg to be allowed through. She was either a very kind woman or we looked desperate because she softened and let us pass, with a better grace than I would have had if I had found two sweaty tramp-like persons in my back garden.

Fortunately our hotel in Rhydycroesau made up for all trials and tribulations. The Pen-y-Dyffryn Hotel welcomed us with tea and scones, a huge, cool room with a bath the size of a swimming pool and wonderful food. I needed it. By this stage the roll call of blisters was as follows: right little toe, right foot ball of foot, left foot under my toes, left foot side, left foot ball of foot, left foot bottom of heel. Ow. Ow, ow, ow. I also had huge scabs on my shoulders where rucksack straps had rubbed and begun to heal. Bob said I looked like a fossil. That helped enormously.

The Pontcysyllte Aqueduct carrying the Llangollen Canal over the River Dee

Chirk Castle

DAY 33 – *Rhydycroesau to Llangollen*

Another scorchingly hot day began, wonderfully, with pancakes and maple syrup for breakfast! As on previous days I discovered that whilst my feet were sore, it was bearable. Just.

However this is a day that you will look forward to and enjoy enormously, weather permitting, since it contains fabulous views, castles, one of Telford's finest achievements, and a halt in a pretty and famous Welsh town.

To achieve the views you have to climb steeply and lengthily out of Rhydycroesau up Selattyn Hill which apparently served as a lookout point in the Second World War, and no wonder. The views from the top are all-encompassing, and on our visit Bob thought he glimpsed the sea on the North Wales coast.

What goes up must come down and it is an equally long descent off the hill towards Chirk, but again what lies at the end is worth the toil. Chirk Castle stands magnificently in rolling parkland high above the River Ceiriog.

One of the chain of Marcher castles built by Edward I to dominate and subdue the Welsh, Chirk was constructed in the late 13th century and occupied by the infamous Roger Mortimer who in later years took Edward II's wife Isabella as his mistress and is accused of murdering the said Edward II at Berkeley Castle, after which he was essentially ruler of England for several years. Inevitably, he came to a sticky end. Since the late 16th century the castle has been owned by the descendants of Sir Thomas Myddelton, who still occupy part of the castle today. The castle is open from March to October and is worth a visit if you have the time. If you just want to see the outside you can do as we did and climb the road steeply to the left and thence down towards Froncysllte, and from here you will have great views to the castle.

The ford in which Helen bathed her feet
at World's End above Llangollen

Looking west towards Maesyrychen Mountain from the Eglwyseg Cliffs

The next highlight of the day was the wonderful, terrifying, Pontcysyllte Aqueduct, which carries the Llangollen canal over the valley of the River Dee at a scary height of 126 feet above the river. It is one of Telford's first engineering masterpieces, is the longest and highest aqueduct in Britain and, deservedly, a World Heritage Site. It is quite scary to walk across as the pathway is narrow, and the drop seems enormous, but you are protected by railings. Not so the canal boats which on the far side have nothing but air beyond the side of the canal.

Finally, on a day of superlatives, we climbed steeply again to reach the famous 'Panorama Walk', a minor road high above the Vale of Llangollen, with far-reaching views to the Cheshire Plain and to Snowdonia in the west. Completing the picturesque end to the day was the ruined Castell Dinas Bran atop its conical hill. It is certain that there was a fortification there in the Iron Age but its main use was by the Princes of Powys as a counterpoint to those Marcher Castles referred to earlier and built by Edward I. Dinas Bran was only occupied by the Welsh for a few decades before the English forced its submission.

Llangollen remains in my memory, unfortunately, as the place where my feet were at their most sore. I remember waking at 5am to go to the bathroom which was only a few steps away and barely being able to make it. I cried, telling Bob, 'I can't walk tomorrow'. The following day, despite a few more tears, I walked 19 miles to Rossett.

DAY 34 – *Llangollen to Rossett*

The section from Llangollen along the Eglwyseg Cliffs to World's End is magnificent. We were lucky enough to do it on a perfect summer morning, with the limestone cliffs shimmering white, dotted here and there with shapely ash and rowan trees, swifts and swallows darting overhead, and a perfect, clear stream of cool water to dip feet into at World's End.

Unfortunately that is pretty much the end of the pleasure on this day. There is then a long, long (and very hot, if it's sunny) walk on a road across Ruabon Moor and Esclusham Mountain, which, if you have sore feet, is very hard! Above Wrexham I confess I cried at the thought of another 10 miles. But it was the prospect of the next 10 miles that brought the tears, not the actual doing of them. One of the things you learn on the Land's End to John O'Groats walk is: once you get over the mental block, the physical part is easy.

On this day Bob did the most amazing job of navigating us through the outskirts of Wrexham. Miraculously, he had found us little paths and snickets that led down to rivers and patches of open fields and green, shady woods along old railway tracks. He made what could have been a terrible slog quite pleasant and interesting.

Fallow herd at Eaton Hall, home of the Duke of Westminster

In one spot we passed an old man sweeping his yard in time to some jazz music he was playing. It was one of those unique moments that become a part of the fantastic kaleidoscope of this entire walk.

Later, desperate for more water on such a hot day, we called into a small shop on a housing estate. The young woman behind the counter found it hard to believe we had walked from Llangollen, but more to the point, she simply could not understand why we would wish to have done so. When we told her that we were walking from Land's End to John O'Groats, she stared blankly at us and asked where that was. We got the feeling that she knew of nothing outside Wrexham, and, worse, was content that it should be so. We felt like aliens, there amongst the anonymous, nondescript suburbs, not belonging and misunderstood.

DAY 35 – *Rossett to Chester*

Suddenly you are in the north. Arrival in Cheshire was another marker on the way. We had walked the south west and Wales and this was most definitely the north, though not yet with the rugged upland beauty that was to come once Manchester was behind us.

Many people might at this point consider a couple of days walking east to reach the Pennine Way in order to follow that route all the way into Scotland but we had our own reasons for our route into Manchester. Firstly, we had both, in the past, walked the full length of the Pennine Way and whilst it is always a delight and an achievement to walk this most special of routes, we wanted to see and walk somewhere different. Secondly, we had it in our minds to walk past the family homes where we had been raised. For Bob this meant walking to Timperley near Altrincham, and for me, the little town of Padiham, further north in Lancashire.

The first aim however was Chester. We chose to cover the first part quickly by walking along a busy road towards Eaton Hall, the country seat of the Duke of Westminster. Having checked that we could walk through his park (he was having an open garden day) and that we could join the River Dee all the way

Apple orchard near Chester

Bob on the trail south of Chester

into Chester, it was a relief to leave the main road. But we were dismayed to find that we could not proceed to the north through the park and gardens without paying a fortune so had to divert round to the south, only then to find that the path by the river was closed here due to a bank collapse (a landslip, not a Northern Rock moment!).

We then had two options: walk a good mile back to the road and find another way or nip over a wall at the back of the mansion and into the gardens. Scandalously, we chose the latter option and subsequently had a lovely peaceful stroll through beautiful gardens until we reached the north gate and finally could join the riverbank path, which was equally delightful. The river was busy with canoes and cruisers, swans and moorhens, and ahead Chester beckoned.

I can recommend the rain which follows a thunderstorm if you have sore feet and legs. We sat on a bench for a rest and after some brief flashes of lightning and a rumble of thunder the heavens opened. Feet and bare legs were held out into the downpour and were most admirably refreshed.

The final stretch into Chester itself meant catching a tiny passenger ferry (actually a motorized rowing boat) across the Dee into the city. You summon the ferry by a quirky sort of semaphore using a bright yellow sign, then sit squeezed up on planks in the bottom of the boat whilst trailing hands in the water as the ferryman put-puts you across - great fun!

We stayed with my niece in Chester that evening and were pampered and cosseted as only family can do!

Crossing the River Dee at Chester

On reflection

In the first month or so of walking we were surprised we saw so few people that it felt as if England had suddenly become depopulated. On many days we walked without encountering another person. It was as if what we were doing was unheard of, and secret. We slipped in and out of towns and hamlets unnoticed and unremarked. It gave us the strangest (and quite pleasant) feeling of being 'non persons'. It came as a bit of a shock when we arrived in Manchester and saw people again!

There were some days on this part of the walk where I was in some considerable pain with my feet.

But who ever said this walk was going to be easy? I think you just have to accept that at times you will be hurting; at times you will not enjoy it. You just have to grit your teeth and get on with it. It's character-forming.

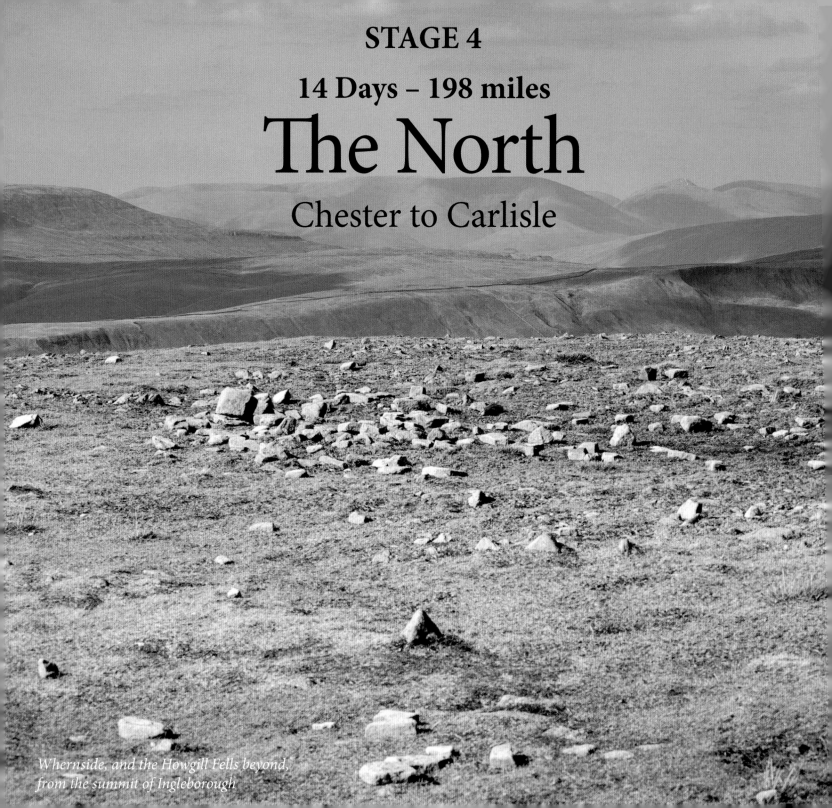

STAGE 4

14 Days – 198 miles
The North
Chester to Carlisle

Whernside, and the Howgill Fells beyond,
from the summit of Ingleborough

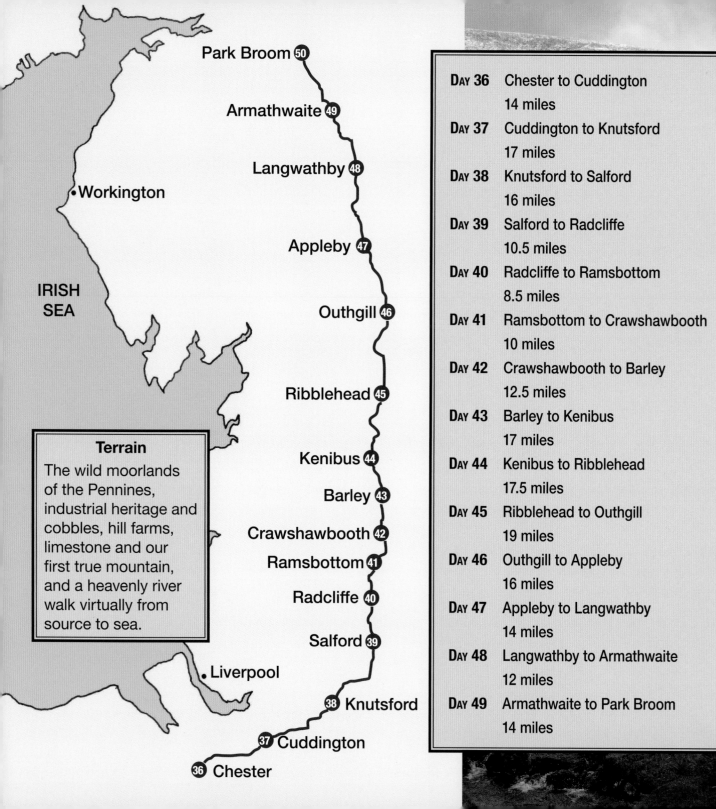

Park Broom 50

Armathwaite 49

Langwathby 48

• Workington

Appleby 47

IRISH
SEA

Outhgill 46

Ribblehead 45

Kenibus 44

Terrain
The wild moorlands of the Pennines, industrial heritage and cobbles, hill farms, limestone and our first true mountain, and a heavenly river walk virtually from source to sea.

Barley 43

Crawshawbooth 42

Ramsbottom 41

Radcliffe 40

Salford 39

• Liverpool

38 Knutsford

37 Cuddington

36 Chester

DAY 36 – *Chester to Cuddington*

Having left the walk in Chester in July we returned to it in September, but were still fortunate with the weather and started out again in warm sunshine.

There was nothing spectacular about this first day, just an easy enough walk through Cheshire's flat arable fields, heading east towards Delamere Forest and ultimately Manchester. In the distance the mass of gantries, chimneys and towers (the chemical works near Frodsham) were spewing clouds of noxious fumes our way. For a mile or so we battled with the sort of smell that burns your throat and coats your tongue. Awful. Being lucky enough to live out in the wilds where the air is relatively clean, we both found it hard to imagine living in close proximity to such fumes. Surely it can't be healthy?

After that, the route improved as we walked down a long green track towards the forest. The damp, rich, earthy scent of the fading summer, the orchards heavy with apples, and the elderberries shiny black in drooping clusters above us, reminded us that autumn was coming.

We had a marvellous treat that evening staying with my sister who cooked us a superb steak in wine followed by delicious apple pie. It was a great return to our walk.

Guelder Rose berries

Day 37 – *Cuddington to Knutsford*

Another day of little drama but pleasant walking. Wherever we walked there seemed to be an abundance of colourful fungi, and even, in one spot, some cyclamen.

Near Cuddington we passed Delamere Park, now a rather posh housing estate but in WWII a huge transit camp for British and American soldiers in the run-up to D-Day.

Later we had a pleasant encounter with some long-eared, soft and friendly donkeys, and a less enjoyable meeting with two large and aggressive farm dogs. Bob informed me that donkeys cannot breed donkeys (something in my ignorance I was not aware of) as a donkey is a cross between a horse and an ass. But a male donkey is an ass, or a jack…. A jackass? And apparently male donkeys are infertile, so how….hang on, I'm missing something here. Perhaps someone will read this and help me out.

Crossing a railway line, the bridge was peppered with graffiti, some of it good, some the usual mindless crudity. I liked *Life is Beatiful* (I assume this was a deliberate spelling mistake).

In many places when walking by rivers and canals we came across that invasive species, Himalayan Balsam. I remember many years ago meeting this invader for the first time by the banks of the River Wye, and hating its un-British appearance and pungent scent. I never imagined then that it would become such a curse of our waterways and even hedgerows. We met it again in huge profusion by the River Weaver, in full bloom and emitting its powerful, rank scent to such an extent that I walked for some way with my scarf over my nose. I fail to understand why the Government is not doing something about this plant. It is changing our riverbanks for ever, for the worse, driving out our native plants and flowers, and nobody seems to be doing anything about it. (See however *The Pocket Guide to Balsam Bashing*.)

The main highlight of the day was watching a canal boat being lifted 50 feet from the River Weaver to the Trent and Mersey Canal via the 150-year-old Anderton Boat Lift. Quite a sight and it must be fairly thrilling if you are on the boat!

The Bridgewater Canal, Sale

Day 38 – *Knutsford to Salford*

If you are thinking of having a day off, Knutsford may be the place to do it. The town itself is pretty, with narrow streets peppered with exclusive shops and delicious eateries, and on the fringe of the town you can walk into Tatton Park with its wide-open acres of parkland, lakes, and herds of deer. Since the town is a favourite haunt of footballers, you can even 'celebrity spot' as you drink your cappuccino.

There was no time for such frivolities for us though. We had Bob's home town of Timperley near Altrincham to visit! We made use of several miles of Tatton Park to get us to the M56 and the edge of Altrincham. On a misty, warm morning, herds of deer appeared like ghosts in the distance, while overhead the planes roared out of Manchester Airport. Suddenly you reach the madness of the motorway that is the M56. Having spent weeks on paths or minor roads, deep in the countryside, motorways are a shock when you come across them. You hear them first, and then, as you stand above them, the speed and the number of vehicles whizzing below you is both startling and mesmeric.

But Timperley was Bob's town and this was Bob's day. To hear his reminiscences, to walk down the streets of his childhood, taught me even more about him. Standing outside his old home, he sensed his parents, long dead, to be very close to him. He told me how as a boy he would sit in the branch of a tree and dream of other places, doing other things – which he has since achieved. It was, for Bob, a happy but almost tearful unlocking of memories, passions and dreams. Our Timperley detour was a very special couple of hours, for both of us.

Trafford Road Bridge

Beetham Tower, Manchester

DAY 39 – *Salford to Radcliffe*

We paused our walk at Salford in September, me with a severely painful hip, so it was a joy to finally get back onto our walk in November, even if the next few stages were only day trips from home! Still fortunate with the weather (bright and sunny), we wound our way out of Manchester through Salford Quays, living proof that something attractive and interesting can come out of a redundant industrial heartland. Striking modern architecture sits comfortably (mostly) side by side with the glorious splendours of Victorian edifices with their scrolls and embellishments.

The leaves not all dead yet, bright red guelder rose berries shining brilliantly in the low sun: you may think that a north Manchester riverside walk towards Bury and Ramsbottom in late autumn doesn't sound full of promise, but you would be wrong. There are still rows of terraced houses and the odd mill chimney but they are attractive and clean now and part of our heritage. However you don't have to walk these streets. The Irwell Sculpture Trail just north of Salford snakes a superb route, away from the noise and bustle of the city, beside the now unpolluted river where geese and swans drift by. Somebody deserves a medal for this. Much of the trail follows disused railway lines, or beside the river. It is quite perfect.

It was here that we met the wonderful old man called Charlie Prince. We'd tailed him mile after mile on the leaf-strewn winding track between Salford and Radcliffe, but, despite his obvious age, we couldn't quite overtake him. He was on his constitutional Sunday walk over a not inconsiderable seven miles for a drink or two with his mates and a ride home on the bus.

Finally we caught up with him, he asked where we were heading and we announced "John O'Groats" and waited for the admiring intake of breath. Charlie's old face gave little away. He wished us well and watched us, heading north, stepping gingerly on the usual sore feet. We paused to photograph tiny white fungus on a mossy bark, and he caught us up again with a "If you don't mind me saying, you two don't look like you could walk to the corner shop!" Those few words haunted us for the rest of the trip and became an almost daily mantra as yet another blister or stiffness caused a wobble to our passage. We of course wanted to be hailed as heroes for walking over 1,100 miles from one end of the country to the other. But Charlie became our hero. He put us in our place, but he also threw down the gauntlet for the remainder of our walk.

DAY 40 – *Radcliffe to Ramsbottom*

Four months since we were last on the walk! Yet again being lucky with the weather, on this day in early March the sun was shining for us once more. Still following the Irwell Sculpture Trail the route wended its way through our industrial past, the heartlands of the Industrial Revolution, clean and quiet now. On the Irwell and the now redundant Manchester Bolton & Bury Canal, noisy Canada Geese were courting loudly, their calls echoing through morning mists; where once narrow boats would have carried coal, only the birds now give life to these waterways.

At Bury Ground we came across the site of the first calico printing works in the UK, built in 1773 and critical to the development of Bury as an industrial town. For the rest of the day we walked past fantastically decorated chimneys still standing proud. My grandmother worked in the mills as a child.

Close to Ramsbottom we came across the heritage East Lancs Railway. Yet another memory intruded when we came across a woman scrubbing her flags (for the uninitiated, this is the pavement outside one's house). One of my jobs as a young child was to help my Grandma "holystone" her flags and lintels which meant being down on your knees with a wet lump of sandstone and scrubbing furiously. The result was spectacularly clean flags and a great deal of pride for the householder. There was not much to celebrate in those tiny houses in grimy streets, but holystoned flags was one of them.

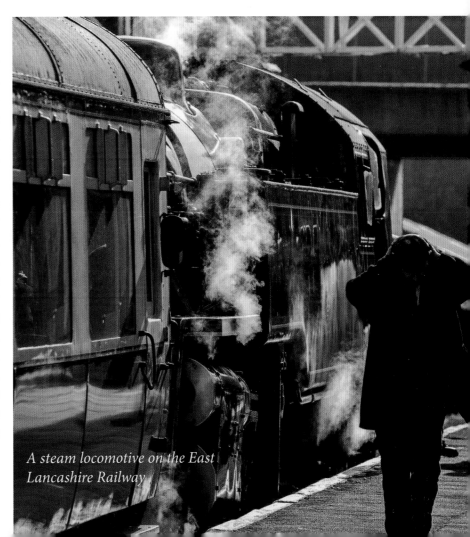

A steam locomotive on the East Lancashire Railway

DAY 41 – *Ramsbottom to Crawshawbooth*

Another warm sunny day saw us still immersed in our industrial past. At Chatterton, in 1826, handloom weavers rioted at the introduction of power looms that they feared, justifiably, would put them out of work. Just to put it into perspective, a weaver who earned six shillings a day in 1792 was earning the same amount for a week of sixteen hour days in 1826. No wonder they rioted. The riots were put down by the military, when 6 people were killed and 69 people arrested. 41 of these were sentenced to death although the sentences were commuted to transportation to Australia. Nothing good came from the riots. Some decent mill owners tried to pay a standard wage but were undercut by other mills, so the poor workers still starved.

However in 1923 after the mill had been demolished the site was donated to the people of Ramsbottom as a Peace Memorial, and is indeed now a beautiful and peaceful place of green fields and trees, with the river burbling quietly by.

I was lucky enough to be brought up in a detached house in the country, but my grandparents were part of this industrial past, and I went to junior school in a mill town where at lunchtimes I would sit on the cobbles by the canal with my back against Mather's Mill wall and listen to the constant hum of the looms inside. That is all gone now, and I have to feel glad that working people today are paid a fair wage for decent hours.

The route we followed was again close by the East Lancs Railway which this time was holding a Diesel weekend, so we did a bit of train-spotting on our walk. We managed to see a train called a Deltic which has the most amazing rumble of sound as it passes by at speed, so it was all fairly exciting. The track side was thronged with real trainspotters too. We called this our Deltic Day.

Some of the place names in the area are unusual to say the least, Ramsbottom being the butt (pardon the pun) of many jokes. However the names mainly originate from Old English or even Norse, so that Ramsbottom actually means "valley of the wild garlic", which is rather pretty, whilst Rawtenstall possibly means "site of an upland farm".

Class 40 Type 4 Diesel (left) and a Class 55 Deltic (right)

We knew without doubt that we were in the North when we reached the equally interestingly named Crawshawbooth, for here we met the first of the rough and wild northern moorlands and came across our first "booth" – a Norse word meaning summer pasture and therefore very much an upland term.

Pendle Hill and the Calder Valley from Hameldon Hill

DAY 42 – *Crawshawbooth to Barley*

The climb out of Crawshawbooth onto Hameldon Hill is particularly steep and will most definitely test your lungs and calves, but the top is worth it for the view northwards towards the higher hills of the Dales and Pennines is spectacular, with the massive bulk of Pendle Hill in the foreground.

On sunny summer days, when I was still at junior school, a special treat was to be taken up to the top of Hameldon Hill and it was as we were walking down a very wet and stony track that I realized this was the same one I had trodden so many years ago as a child. I won't state here quite how many years ago that was, but it was a lot! I recall that it felt very adventurous at the time, and seems quite tame now, but perhaps it was the beginning of a love for the outdoors that has never waned.

It was on this day that it was my turn to be nostalgic for we were walking though the village where I went to school, into my home town, and up the hill to my parent's house where my Mum was waiting for us with a cup of tea and a bowl of icy water (for the sore feet).

The first village was Hapton, where my maternal grandparents lived, a plain, industrial village of terraces and old mills, mostly now demolished or converted, and from there it was down across the moor to Padiham,

my home town. There is nothing special about Padiham, except to me. I can't say make sure you visit it, for there is nothing particularly remarkable to see, but I am proud of it. We walked past the wonderful 1930s town hall, with its art deco interior and marble steps, where my Dad used to work and I attended my first ever disco, up to St Leonard's Church where I was baptized in a 1525 stone font, more climbing up the steep hill called Moor Lane which has rubber strips inserted in the pavement to stop people slipping and which was my walk home from school, and finally across the new bypass and out into the country to the house my Dad designed and built. For an hour or so my heart was full, moved, emotional. May you find such special days on your own walk.

This was the end of the industrial scenery that had been our companion since Manchester. Now the mill chimneys and terraced streets gave way to small country villages huddled under the steep moors and surrounded by fine green pastures. At Higham and beyond into the villages under Pendle you will come across the story of the Lancashire Witches. In 1612 twelve people from the Pendle area were charged with witchcraft and tried at Lancaster Assizes. One died in prison, ten were executed, and one found not guilty. There are reminders throughout the area, including a long distance path from Sabden to Lancaster and a shop called Witches Galore!

DAY 43 – *Barley to Kenibus*

At the end of March we set out from Barley to walk home to our house called Kenibus, north of Slaidburn. Snow was lying thickly on the northern slopes of Pendle but the sun was out, lambs were in the fields and the first part of the walk out of Barley followed a wonderfully clear stream right to the foot of the "big end" of Pendle, which is one of the steepest climbs you

are likely to encounter on your walk. It is severe! At the top, some 1827 feet up, an incredible vista opens up of the route northwards. To the north and east the magnificent Yorkshire three peaks of Pen-y-ghent, Ingleborough and Whernside rise beyond the green of the Ribble valley, whilst directly in front the lonely uplands of the Forest of Bowland swell up, with the sea glinting in the far distance below the Lake District mountains. Turn the other way to review your route and on a clear day you see Liverpool and the mountains of Snowdonia beyond. Pendle is not to be missed.

Below Pendle on the north side is one of the prettiest villages you can imagine. The stone cottages of Downham huddle around a duck-dabbled beck and line the steep lane up to the church at the top. There are no yellow lines on the roads, no satellite dishes, no TV aerials, no obtrusive signs. It is a village preserved in aspic by the Assheton family who have owned it since the 16th century, and as such it has been the setting for several historical TV dramas.

From one estate village to another, you arrive in Slaidburn, a historic, unspoiled and pretty dales village through which the River Hodder flows across a village green and where you can get the best mug of tea and fresh cakes at the tiny Riverbank Tearooms.

And finally we arrived home. There is nothing quite like opening your own front door at the end of a long and hard walk, lighting the fire, having a bath, and sleeping in your own bed. Wonderful! And a landmark. We had walked from Land's End to Kenibus. If we managed no more, that was an achievement to be proud of in any case. But there was more to come…

DAY 44 – *Kenibus to Ribblehead*

If you are following the same route then you will not be starting from Kenibus since that was our home, but you could start out from our new home just half a mile away at Merrybent Hill, where we now run a luxury B&B! Whatever your start point, be prepared for a very long and hard day, with a climb over your first real mountain and a series of ascents which in total amount to over 3,500 feet.

We set out on a frosty sunny morning with lambs frolicking in our neighbour's fields and the lapwings calling overhead to celebrate their spring return to the uplands. It was a morning for joy as we climbed out of our valley to stand proudly on top of Catlow Fell and look back to our house nestled by the wood, Pendle in the distance, Stocks Reservoir just below us gleaming in the sun. For us, on such a perfect morning in the place we love the most, it was a highlight of our entire walk.

Pen-y-ghent seen from Bowland Knotts

Onwards and upwards however! Crossing the long open moor towards Clapham the bulk of Ingleborough rears up, becoming larger and more dominant with every step. By the time you are beneath it, it seems enormous.

At Clapham you are in true Yorkshire Dales limestone country. If you have time on the route up pay a quick visit to Ingleborough Caves which display magnificent examples of stalactites and stalagmites in an underground wonderland. Then there is an exciting scramble up through Trow Gill, a narrow limestone ravine which drips with moisture, before emerging onto the slopes of Ingleborough for the final pull to the top where there are more startling views. Though on our visit there was snow lying and a bitterly cold gale blowing, so we didn't linger!

On the way up you may want to divert briefly to see Gaping Gill, a 322 feet deep pothole and one of the largest in Britain. The climb down the other side of Ingleborough is tricky. There is a route but it is extremely steep, poorly pitched, and requires some caution for the first half mile. I confess I complained bitterly most of the way down. The reward as you descend is stunning limestone scenery all about you, crowned by the magnificence of the Ribblehead Viaduct at the head of the valley and your destination. If you are lucky you may see a steam train crossing the viaduct – it is a great sight.

DAY 45   – Ribblehead to Outhgill

I haven't mentioned my blisters for a while, so here's an update. They were still there, still huge, still very painful. No change there then. It was still a case of grit teeth and walk. And this day was a long one, 19 miles up through the dales into the Eden Valley, on a grey, wet day. But what scenery, even in the mist! The route basically follows the line of the Settle-Carlisle Railway, which simply has to be one of the most magnificent train journeys in the UK. In most places we walked above the line, passing the highest mainline railway station in the country at Dent, and onwards over lonely, empty moors to drop down into Garsdale where we had a nice rest in the warm waiting room at Garsdale station.

There is an interesting little memorial here, to a dog called Ruswarp, who signed the petition to save the Settle-Carlisle Line with his pawprint and who stayed by his master's side for 11 weeks when his master sadly died out in the hills in Wales.

On our way over the moor we met two dry-stone wallers and had a chat to them. It is such a skilled, (and never ending!) job and on many occasions on our walk we admired the various styles and beauties of the dry stone walls that stretched across the landscape and which are so peculiarly British.

The Mallerstang valley, from Garsdale all the way to Kirkby Stephen, is to be savoured. The young River Eden has its source high up above Mallerstang Edge on your right and is fed by becks tumbling down from the distinctive Wild Boar Fell on your left, and you will follow this beautiful and unspoilt river as it grows and matures virtually all the way from source to sea near Carlisle. It will be a very beautiful section of your walk.

*Left: Ribblehead viaduct
with snow-covered
Whernside in the distance.*

Right: The North Pennines

DAY 46 – *Outhgill to Appleby-in-Westmorland*

This was probably the worst day of the whole walk for me and the one occasion when I actually questioned why I was doing this. There was one reason for this, the state of my feet and body! That morning my feet were extremely painful, more blisters developed during the day, and for some reason my socks were causing a painful, itchy red rash around my ankles. Things couldn't have been much worse, but we had a day off planned once we got to Appleby, so it was simply a case of getting there. It did mean that I didn't appreciate the scenery as much as I should have done!

There is a dramatic start as you pass by Pendragon Castle, a picturesque ruin reputedly built by Uther Pendragon of Tintagel fame (though what he was doing up here goodness knows) but actually the castle was built by the Normans in the 12th century.

You may also come across many ponies in the fields and the fells around Appleby, which is the site for the unique Horse Fair that occurs in June every year and attracts over 10,000 Gypsies and Travellers. If you want to see the fair then plan well ahead as accommodation will be in very short supply.

Below: Mallerstang Edge from near Outhgill *Right: Market day in Appleby-in-Westmorland*

The views as we walked northwards up the valley towards Appleby were stunning. On our right the long range of the snow covered Pennines stretched across the country, the great scar of High Cup Nick cutting into the fells, then Great Dun Fell with its golf ball radar station, and finally the high point of the Pennines, Cross Fell, which would be our companion for the next day or so as we headed north.

If you have decided to take the Pennine Way on your route north you will be on top of these fells looking down on the Eden Valley! You may also hear artillery and gunfire from the military ranges at Warcop. How odd, Bob said, to simultaneously hear the sounds of war and the sounds of birdsong. How strange, and how lucky, not to feel fear at the sounds of war. To the left but more distant the blue shadowed peaks of the Lake District were an invitation for another day and another walk.

Appleby – a rest day

We had a day off in Appleby and if you are ready for a break too then this is a perfect spot. The town itself is very pretty, medieval and Georgian houses and quaint shops stretching up the steep tree-lined main street from the church at the bottom to be crowned by the castle at the summit. It used to be the county town of the old county of Westmorland, and until 1974 was simply called Appleby but the name was changed in that year as a way of preserving the name of the old county. The castle itself was founded in the early 12th century, as was the church at the bottom of the hill, and parts of the tower dating from that period remain.

Other than these charms, the River Eden runs through the centre of the town (to the town's detriment, when there are severe floods as happened in December 2015), and there are several short walks which can be taken around the town and by the river. At the top of the town the Settle-Carlisle Railway passes through so you could take a trip on that for the day if your feet and legs feel like they need a proper rest.

Day 47 – *Appleby-in-Westmorland to Langwathby*

The good news on this day was that my feet were feeling better, I was refreshed and ready and willing to walk again. Amazing what a little rest and a break can do. Even 20 minutes for coffee and a sandwich on the walk can turn you from tired and aching to raring to go again, and the miraculous effects of dipping feet in a stream or the sea are to be seen to be believed.

Our main route out of Appleby was following a Roman road through some trees for several miles, and after that a series of tiny quiet country roads at the foot of the Pennines to our right, followed by another Roman road, which, notably, was extremely straight and therefore felt long! The little villages we passed through were pretty and so rural that in fact passing through one farmyard we were ankle-deep in cow poo.

Accommodation being in short supply we caught the train at Langwathby to our hotel in Armathwaite where we were staying for two nights (the Fox and Pheasant, lovely).

Day 48 – *Langwathby to Armathwaite*

Starting the day with a short train ride back to Langwathby was quite pleasant as it allowed us to wake up and prepare ourselves gently for once instead of the usual get up, breakfast, check out, walk.

On a beautiful spring morning, with sparrows chattering busily in the bushes, we walked along the side of the Eden above the flood plain with a steep drop here and there to the river and periodic evidence of where flooding and torrents had undercut the bank severely. Even here deep in the country there was evidence of past industry, with the rusting remains of old railways and shafts by the side of the track where gypsum, used in plaster and as a fertilizer, was mined and in fact is still mined today in nearby Kirkby Thore.

However the walk beside the river can only be described as outstanding in all respects; whether we were right on the bank or high above it, the scenery, punctuated by the swift but silent waters, was a microcosm of England at its best. Wooded hills, green fields dotted with sheep, airy walkways above steep valleys, sweeping pastures reaching up to a perfect cerulean sky.

To add to the interest, at Lacy's Caves you come across shapely caves cut into the local red sandstone and looking out over the river. It would be nice to believe these were the haunt of some medieval hermit, and if so he could not have chosen a better spot, but no, these caves were in fact created in the 18th century by an obviously eccentric local landowner, who had the area planted with ornamental gardens and used to entertain friends to dinner there.

Just off the route and most definitely worth a brief visit if you have the time can be found Long Meg and Her Daughters, which are a genuine ancient monument, being a Bronze Age stone circle. As with all other monuments of this type, no one knows for certain why they were constructed, but there is no doubt at all that on a quiet evening as the sun goes down there is a mysteriousness and a presence about these stones which wakens some primeval instinct in us all.

There is so much to see and enjoy on this day that you may find yourself lingering too long here and there. Kirkoswald village is another delightful site which may tempt you. The church here, parts of which are 12th century, has, uniquely, a 19th century bell tower situated on top of a little mound above the river some 200 yards away from the church itself, probably so that villagers could hear the bell more clearly.

Finish the day with an airy stroll high above the river with stunning views back down the gorge, then drop down into Coombs Wood for a sylvan stroll into Armathwaite. If you have the good fortune to experience that clear, delicately warm spring sunshine as we did, then this will be a day to remember for a long time.

Little Salkeld Watermill

99

The River Eden at Warwick Bridge

DAY 49 – *Armathwaite to Park Broom*

This will be another day of riverside delights as you will follow the Eden, this time mostly on the left bank, all the way north to Carlisle.

There were more ups and downs on this day as the path we took climbed away from the river then would drop steeply to rejoin it, then climb again, but what became noticeable today was the way the river was gradually changing, becoming wide and smooth, and of such different character from the tumbling torrent we first knew in Mallerstang. Here there are islands in the river, occupied at the time of our visit by noisy wild geese with pretty orange bills and feet (Greylag Geese, we think), whilst fishermen were casting their lines and we were even fortunate enough to see a kingfisher flash close by us in a shock of electric blue.

At Wetheral you come across the genuine article in terms of hermits' dwellings! St Constantine's Cells lie above the river and were used by monks as early as the 14th century, though for refuge not reflection. The village itself is very pretty and has an almost foreign feel to is as you come across its large green surrounded by large and ornate houses in many different styles.

We crossed the river again here via a very high footpath running next to the 100 feet high Wetheral Railway Viaduct, and that marked a turning point in river and scenery, for both were very different afterwards, the river widening and slowing even further to spread out across a broad floodplain where flood debris of uprooted trees and branches dotted the flat fields and hundreds of sand martins swooped and switched back and forth across the creamy brown water.

On reflection

Unfortunately at Salford I had a problem with my hip that was so severe I thought I had possibly dislocated it, and I couldn't even climb a kerb. There was no question of gritting teeth and bearing it this time, I simply could not walk. But by the end of this section we felt we had really achieved something.

We had crossed Bob's home county, and mine, we had travelled from the border of Wales to within striking distance of Scotland, we had survived the sorest of feet and the scorn of Charlie Prince, and my hip had recovered. We had walked through memories, passed beyond the Pennines, followed a beautiful river from source almost to sea. We had walked across England and Wales. And we had been together through it all.

Lacy's Caves on the River Eden

Primroses and celandines in a churchyard, Warwick Bridge

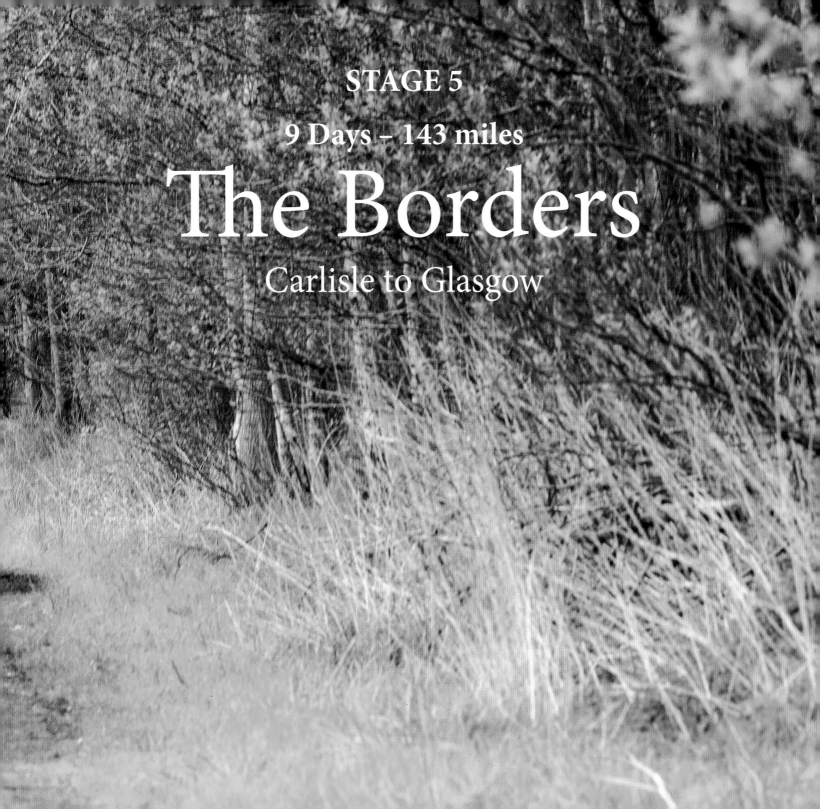

STAGE 5

9 Days – 143 miles

The Borders

Carlisle to Glasgow

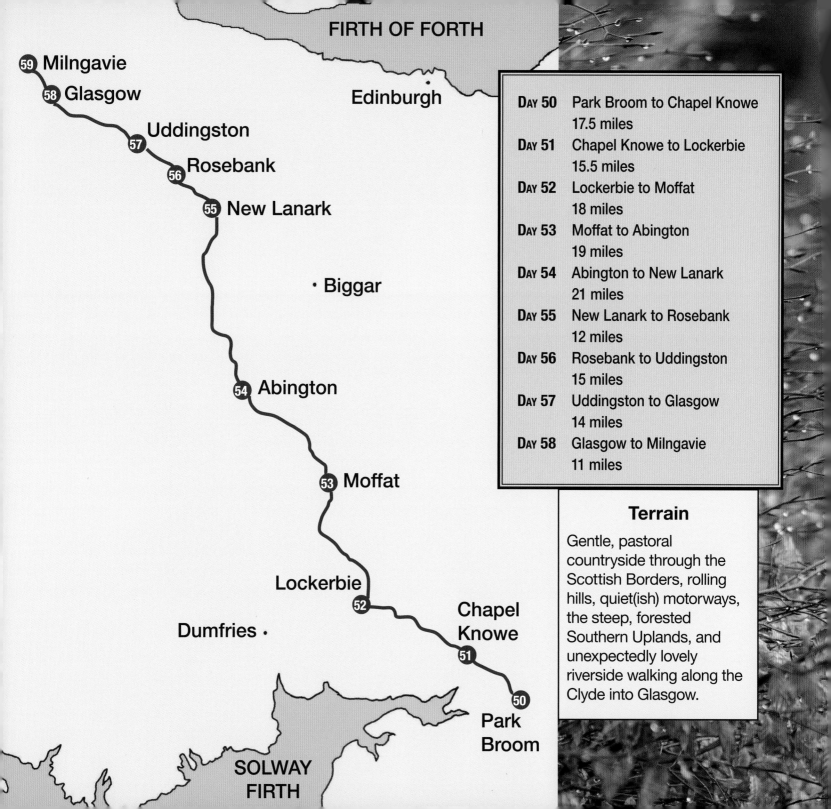

FIRTH OF FORTH

59 Milngavie
58 Glasgow
Edinburgh
Uddingston
57
56 Rosebank
55 New Lanark

· Biggar

54 Abington

53 Moffat

Lockerbie
Dumfries ·
52
Chapel Knowe
51
50
Park Broom

SOLWAY FIRTH

DAY 50	Park Broom to Chapel Knowe 17.5 miles
DAY 51	Chapel Knowe to Lockerbie 15.5 miles
DAY 52	Lockerbie to Moffat 18 miles
DAY 53	Moffat to Abington 19 miles
DAY 54	Abington to New Lanark 21 miles
DAY 55	New Lanark to Rosebank 12 miles
DAY 56	Rosebank to Uddingston 15 miles
DAY 57	Uddingston to Glasgow 14 miles
DAY 58	Glasgow to Milngavie 11 miles

Terrain

Gentle, pastoral countryside through the Scottish Borders, rolling hills, quiet(ish) motorways, the steep, forested Southern Uplands, and unexpectedly lovely riverside walking along the Clyde into Glasgow.

DAY 50 – *Park Broom to Chapel Knowe*

This is a momentous day. Today you will cross the line of Hadrian's Wall, cross the River Esk, and shortly after, you arrive in Scotland. After weeks of walking, your ultimate destination seems a lot closer, for this is your final country at last. Don't be fooled: you still have a long, long way to go and the Highlands to traverse. Nevertheless, this is a day to savour.

You may have decided to walk into Carlisle itself instead of bypassing it as we did, and the city does deserve a visit. It was the main Roman settlement in the north though there are few, if any, visible signs of that today, but the magnificent 11th century castle and the old centre of the city are worth a look. Otherwise your way points west and north across flat flood plains towards Longtown and the border.

The walking was not particularly exciting on the whole, wending our way on quiet country roads through flat fields sprouting pylons, once we had got past the M6 and away from the very busy A7.

The River Esk at Longtown

The wind blowing off the Solway Firth was strong and icy, unhindered by hills, so finding anywhere to sit with a cup of coffee without freezing proved troublesome but eventually we managed a break in a peaceful spot that was apparently the site of the Battle of Solway Moss in 1542 when the Scots were routed by the English.

Once through the rather characterless town of Longtown, whose two main claims to fame are the possession of the largest sheep market in England, and one of the largest ammunition depots in Europe, our way continued on quiet wooded lanes. The Scottish border was a milestone we had long anticipated. We imagined ourselves standing beneath a huge sign that said *Welcome to Scotland* but in fact as we were on the back roads there was no sign at all! The best we could manage was an old date stone on a tiny bridge which said Cumberland on one side and Dumfriesshire on the other. I don't even have a photograph as it was too obscured to be worth it. Nevertheless, we were in Scotland!

Be aware of the extreme shortage of accommodation in this area. You need to plan ahead and ensure that you have somewhere to go and something to eat. We were lucky enough to find a marvellous B&B at Torbeckhill, where the owner came to pick us up, cooked us a wonderful dinner, and took us back the following morning.

DAY 51 – *Chapel Knowe to Lockerbie*

A wet, wet day! To add to the joys, I received an insect bite at Armathwaite which by the time I got to Chapel Knowe was angry, swollen, and most uncomfortable. When I finally managed to see a doctor, it appeared my leg was infected and I was immediately put onto antibiotics. The trials and tribulations of walking!

This was another day when it felt as if we were the last people in the country. The quiet lanes were empty of traffic, and even the pretty little village of Eaglesfield was deserted. Then we climbed. And climbed. And climbed! Not very steeply, not achieving great height, and actually a pleasant change after the flatness of the Solway fields.

It was a relief to walk the long hill down into Lockerbie and find a welcome cup of tea in a café, for we were wet, cold and tired and my swollen leg had become very painful.

Lockerbie of course is sadly known for the terrorist disaster when Pan Am Flight 103 exploded over the town, killing all on board and 11 residents of Lockerbie. There is a memorial garden to the victims on the outskirts of the town.

This was the end of one section of walking so we caught the Settle-Carlisle train back home in the early evening, when we were fortunate enough that the sun came out and we were treated to some of the most magnificent light on the Pennines and the Dales as the train retraced our route down the Eden valley.

Looking towards the Southern Uplands from just south of Moffat

DAY 52 – *Lockerbie to Moffat*

On another beautifully sunny day in April we walked out of Lockerbie, impressed to spot they had both an ice rink and a squash court, most unusual!

You would think that walking beside a motorway for miles would be highly unpleasant but in fact it was much better than expected. Of course, this isn't exactly the M25, and despite a degree of traffic noise we were still able to hear blackbirds singing and, to make our day, we saw the first swallow. I know, one swallow doesn't make a summer…. but it was a harbinger of better days to come.

You may wonder why anyone would choose to walk beside a motorway but in fact there is little choice on this section. The alternative would be to walk east or west in a zig-zag pattern, still on roads, so our decision was, head due north!

At either Johnstonebridge or Beattock you can decide to turn away from the motorway onto quiet country roads. Despite my assurances above, it was a welcome relief to suddenly find the background drone of traffic has miraculously disappeared.

By now the landscape has begun to change again for you are on the edge of the swelling Southern Uplands; great rolling humps of green swoop down to the pretty waters of the River Annan besides which Moffat nestles in a sheltered bowl in the hills.

This is an attractive spa town of handsome, grand stone houses, between which there are airy views to the surrounding hills, and it possesses an unusual double main street lined with pollarded trees. You can still visit the well which supplied sulphurous water to the bath house (now the Town Hall).

DAY 53 – *Moffat to Abington*

The Annandale Way led us quietly out of Moffat on a buddingly leafy lane heading arrow-straight for the gloriously named Devil's Beef Tub at the head of the valley. The hills around Moffat feel more like Shropshire than Scotland as they do not have that rugged sharpness of the Highlands but instead are rounded and broad. If you blindfolded me then dropped me on the Annandale Way and asked me where I was, I could as easily say Craven Arms as Moffat. Regardless of that, and the nearby motorway, the sections through the Southern Uplands, on breezy, sunny spring days, were a real pleasure to walk. A Roman road leading north is marked on the map which we wanted very much to follow but in fact there is little evidence of it on the ground so we turned away from the Beef Tub to cross the hills on a small B road and wend our way back to the motorway again!

We have spent many days over the years driving the M74 on our way to and from a cottage we own on the Isle of Skye, so we are very familiar with the scenery, but only by walking a land do you begin to really know it and discover its secrets. Sitting high above the motorway and then following it all the way into Crawford and beyond, we came across beautiful little waterfalls, while lime green silver birch shimmers, clinging to the banks and wrens and dippers flit above the water. Nature manages its own way very well, despite the presence only yards away of concrete and tarmac.

The first sight of the River Clyde South of Crawford

These hills are the birthplace of two great rivers: to the east the River Tweed rises from the Devil's Beef Tub and heads east to the North Sea, whilst behind us as we walked the magnificent River Clyde has its source, and shortly after Beattock Summit, we met it briefly. It then heads off in a wide loop before turning west towards Lanark, where we would join it again to accompany it all the way into Glasgow. Seeing the Clyde was another significant moment in our walk. We had to pinch ourselves a little and kept repeating with a sort of stunned wonder: "This is the Clyde! We've walked from Land's End to the Clyde!"

Struggling for accommodation we booked a tiny B&B at a village called Roberton, and again we had the help of the owner who came to collect us, offered us two bathrooms to use, made wonderful tea and scones, and cooked us a roast chicken dinner followed by spotted dick! So many times on the walk, moments like that, when people put themselves out, made such a difference to us. Very often it restored our faith in human nature.

DAY 54 – *Abington to New Lanark*

When you are driving the M74 and you reach Abington, you know that Glasgow is just round the corner and you will be there in forty minutes or so. I think we subconsciously had this in our minds when we left Abington, and it came as something of a shock that, 21 miles later and with very tired legs, we still had another three days long walking to do before we reached the centre of Glasgow. Be prepared, then, for a long hard day on your walk to New Lanark!

Climbing steadily out of Abington on a good cycle track away from the M74, the scenery became brownly bleak as we passed Red Moss and Black Burn on our left. Pylons marched steadily across the open moor, an icy wind blew into our faces, and still we climbed. Far ahead we could see a building that was marked as a hotel on the map, so we dreamed of stopping there to perhaps sit by a log fire with a nice cup of tea before proceeding on our way. Oh dear, no! It turned out to be a rather grim-looking truck stop which we didn't fancy at all!

There were not many occasions on the walk when we were bored but for one or two miles on this stretch we needed a bit of a diversion so first Bob started making funny shadows for me to guess at (his John Wayne was rather good), then we played a game where we had to guess the colour and make of the car coming up behind us. Somehow Bob rapidly claimed he was 22-1 up. I'm not suggesting there was any cheating going on here but…..

At Happendon we at last said farewell to the M74. There is a good cycle route into Glasgow through Lesmahagow and Hamilton, but we particularly wanted to visit New Lanark and thence follow the Clyde all the way into Glasgow so we turned off here to wend our way east along Douglas Water through a strange landscape of fields interspersed with opencast mines and grassed-over slag heaps.

Finally we rejoined the Clyde where it begins to tumble and roar its way through a narrow wooded gorge. The area is known as the Falls of Clyde, and whilst I had expected perhaps one waterfall, in fact the couple of miles down the gorge can only be described as awesome!

As it was Easter Monday, the path along the gorge became increasingly busy but this couldn't detract from the delights of the many falls, where mini rainbows formed in the sun sparkling on misty droplets, and birds twittered and flitted between lime green trees soaring up from the shadows to the blue sky above the gorge. We were even treated to the amazing sight of a peregrine falcon sitting on her nest across the gorge. There was a viewing station and a Ranger lent us a telescope and pointed the bird out to us, otherwise the camouflage of the grey feathers against the shadowed stone would have made her impossible to see.

You then find yourself in the stunning World Heritage Site of New Lanark. Perfectly preserved mills, tenement housing and waterwheels sit picturesquely on the banks of the Clyde. Founded in 1785 for cotton milling, it became an example of a

The Falls of Clyde, New Lanark

New Lanark World Heritage Site

planned settlement operating under the principles of Utopian Socialism, under the management of Robert Owen, who was also one of the founders of the cooperative movement.

At New Lanark he opened the first infants' school in Britain. New Lanark is also famous as the birthplace of David Livingstone. There is a hotel in the restored mills but unfortunately we didn't stay there: we walked another mile or so up and out of the gorge towards Lanark itself where we stayed at the very odd Scottish Equi B&B, a series of wooden buildings alongside a horseriding complex. It wasn't bad, though not the luxury advertised on their website.

Then the bistro of our choice was closed and we had to walk again to get something to eat, so with sore feet and feeling utterly weary, I am terribly ashamed to say that once in our room I wailed a little. (Bob would say a lot.)

Below: Looking north near Red Moss, north of Abington

DAY 55 – *New Lanark to Rosebank*

We joined the Clyde Walkway which we followed for the next few days right into the centre of Glasgow. When someone mentions The Clyde, what do you think of? Shipyards, industry, backstreets, grimness, impenetrable accents? I did. How wrong I was (except for the accents). Up and down through a gentle gorge, through woods heady with the scent of bluebells and wild garlic, past yet more waterfalls, and the treat of yet another kingfisher dashing right past our noses! It was actually idyllic.

Occasionally there was evidence of what the Clyde can do in spate. There were many bank collapses and in one spot, just yards away from a house, a whole section of bank, carrying mature trees with it, had slipped forward in a collapse that would have undoubtedly destroyed the building had it hit. Bob reminded me how, on our trek on the South West Coast Path (how long ago that seems), we had said silent prayers pleading for the path to NOT collapse as we walked it!

The River Clyde, New Lanark

Day 56 – *Rosebank to Uddingston*

A green, spring-scented day. Everything sparkled fresh and clean after a night of rain. Still following the bucolic corridor of the Clyde between increasingly suburban hinterlands, we passed a hugely busy road junction before emerging onto the flood plain of the Clyde close to the atmospheric, neo-gothic ruin of Cambusnethan House.

In the distance the quirky modern architecture of Muirhouse flats was a reminder that the city was nearby. If you have driven south on the M74 out of Glasgow, you will recognize these tower blocks - the ones with the odd multi-coloured owls on top. I hope I never have to find out what it is like to live on the 17th floor of one of these monstrosities.

One of the great things about walking is that you feel intimately connected with the earth. You notice the little things. Beside the Clyde there were minute little metallic green beetles, immaculately crafted minuscule snails, petals, buds, leaves, bark, stamens, stalks, sand martins, cormorants drying their wings….all of the things that go unnoticed when you are flying past in a car.

On the Clyde Walkway

Just outside Motherwell you walk through an RSPB reserve, though we wouldn't have known it, before arriving at the lovely, though artificial, Strathclyde Loch. Another sunny day so it was busy with canoeists and little sailing boats whilst people strolled on the circuit path as they enjoyed the (very) fresh air.

Our final section of the day followed the Clyde through elegant Bothwell back into woods beside the river before reaching the red ruins of 13th century Bothwell Castle defending a bend high above the river, another unexpected encounter on our journey along the Clyde.

Day 57 – *Uddingston to Glasgow*

Little accommodation in Uddingston so we stayed in Glasgow and caught a train back to the village in the morning. We found ourselves walking above the wooded river valley through a strange 'no man's land' of open ground, grassed over spoil heaps, froths of blackthorn blossom, with, to our delight, a herd of roe deer grazing calmly on the open ground. So close to the city, yet nature still finds a way to survive. Even though

Mauldslie Bridge over the Clyde at Rosebank

117

the Clyde Walkway was increasingly urban, in that occasionally we could see new housing nearby, and the path was now tarmac, it nevertheless remained a secret, hidden, green corridor sneaking us quietly into Glasgow.

There were some indications however that we were no longer in the heart of the country. We had a forced detour from the path into the suburbs, caused by a bank collapse. Here we suddenly realized that we were in a large and not always safe city. Through quarter of a mile of streets we passed through an area of scrap merchants, traveller encampments, burnt-out cars, and rusty factories.

For the first and only time on the walk we did not feel safe. Even on return to the river we came across a car upended in the water, and another, burnt, in the woods. We sat on a bench for a quick break and realised it was a sad memorial to a young boy of 16 who had drowned in the river. The bench carried the photograph of a young, smiling, handsome face, a 'bonny lad' . Such a waste of a life.

Closer into the city we came across the site of the athletes' housing for the Glasgow Commonwealth Games. Hundreds of brand new flats were built around the Commonwealth Arena. Hopefully this attractive new housing will continue to regenerate a run-down area.

And then, finally, we were in Glasgow proper, popping out of our leafed corridor

Bothwell Castle, Uddingston

into the wide open spaces of the lovely Glasgow Green. On the river, a young woman rowed swiftly through the sparkling water, couples strolled, walking dogs, along the flower-lined paths through turfed lawns, and friendly police cycled past, enjoying the sunshine.

Here you will find the magnificent People's Palace and Winter Gardens. Opened in 1898, its purpose was 'to be a palace of pleasure and imagination' as a relief from the grim Victorian life people lived in the overcrowded East End of Glasgow. Today it is a living museum detailing how the people of Glasgow lived, whilst the Winter Gardens, inside a huge conservatory, is a warm and exotic stroll through plants and palms.

Above: Blackthorn blossom near Uddingston and (below) we surprised some roe deer

The Clyde can be followed all the way to where it meets the Firth of Clyde beyond Dumbarton, and if we had had time we would have liked to do this, but central Glasgow beckoned. This is one of our greatest cities, once the largest seaport in Britain and famous for its shipbuilding which still continues today. Rough and ready in parts, with inhabitants who appear to be speaking a foreign language, the city nevertheless charms you with its Victorian grandeur, culture, architecture and friendliness.

Above: St Andrew's Suspension Bridge, Glasgow Green and (right) skunk cabbages at Milngavie

DAY 58 – *Glasgow to Milngavie*

We end this chapter of our walk at Milngavie (pronounced Mullguy), since this is the outer extent of Glasgow and the point where you begin to leave central Scotland and the lowlands behind and embark on the West Highland Way, which will lead you to the very foot of Ben Nevis, Britain's highest mountain.

Just because it is so famous, we walked out of Glasgow up Sauchiehall Street, past the Glasgow School of Art with its Charles Rennie Mackintosh exterior, and then plunged, hobbit-like, below the streets to find the secret

walkway which is our exit from the city. The Kelvin Walkway does as the Clyde Walkway did, and threads quietly through the city, a hidden gem of river and trees below the noisy streets.

Unfortunately that is probably the best part of it. Once the Kelvin Walkway emerges from the city it becomes a muddy track beside the river, through rather uninspiring countryside, though it does cross the northernmost frontier of the Roman Empire, the Antonine Wall, which we were hoping to see some evidence of, but didn't.

Closer to Milngavie we left the River Kelvin for a smaller stream which we named Trolley River for its huge crop of discarded and rusting shopping carts. Growing beside the water were huge yellow flowers which we subsequently discovered were skunk cabbage, not native to the UK, very poisonous and definitely to be avoided. They seemed appropriate, however, in their wasteland environment.

On reflection

The main sensation of this section of the walk was surprise. Having expected that the walk from Carlisle to Glasgow would be an uninspiring drag, we instead fell in love with Moffat and the surrounding scenery, treasured our secret walk along the length of the Clyde, and ended up in a wonderful, vibrant Scottish city. We learnt on this section that simply to explore unfamiliar areas with an open mind can lead to as much pleasure as walking through the more classically beautiful parts of our country. Apart from the one dodgy section, we would happily walk the Clyde again.

Glasgow also marked another significant step on the walk. England was well behind us, so were the Scottish Lowlands, and the last major city. From this point on we turned our faces towards the Highlands and scented the wind blowing from John O'Groats. We left Glasgow with the feeling that we were nearly there, on the last leg, so much already accomplished and behind us but with perhaps the best yet to come…

The footpath towards Ben Nevis crosses the slopes of Meall an t-Suidhe

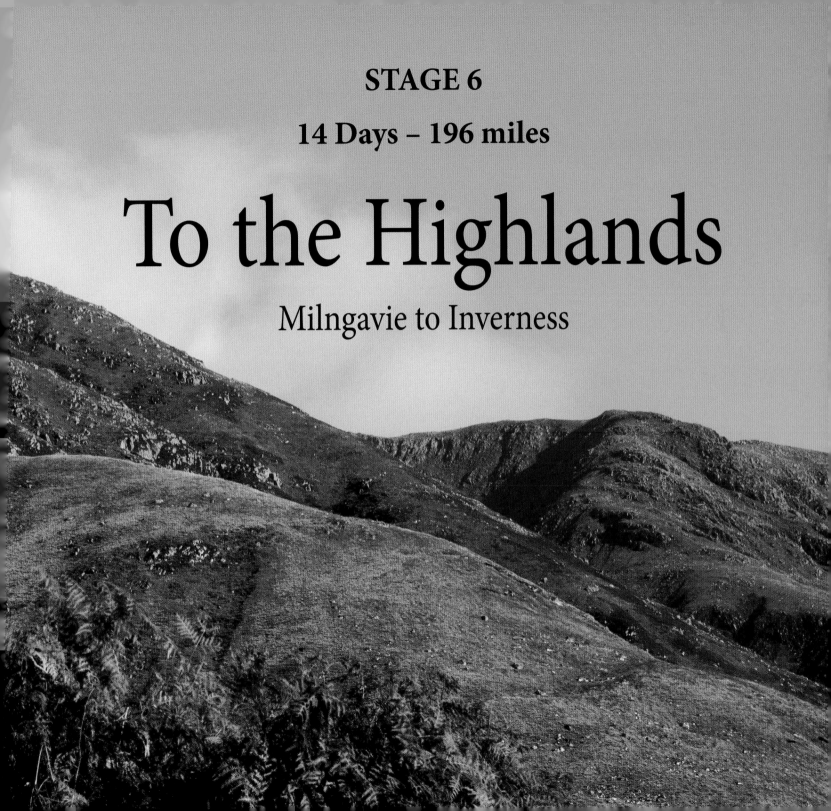

STAGE 6

14 Days – 196 miles

To the Highlands

Milngavie to Inverness

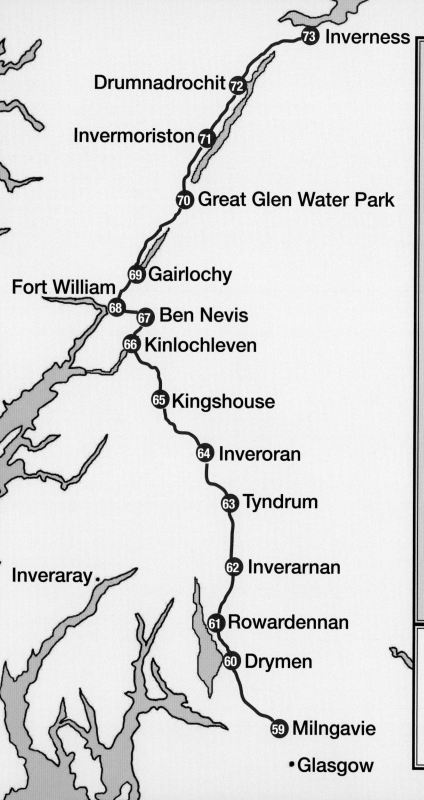

DAY 59	Milngavie to Drymen	13 miles
DAY 60	Drymen to Rowardennan	14 miles
DAY 61	Rowardennan to Inverarnan	16 miles
DAY 62	Inverarnan to Tyndrum	13 miles
DAY 63	Tyndrum to Inveroran	10 miles
DAY 64	Inveroran to Kingshouse	11 miles
DAY 65	Kingshouse to Kinlochleven	10 miles
DAY 66	Kinlochleven to Fort William	13 miles
DAY 67	Ben Nevis	15.5 miles. 4600 feet up!
DAY 68	Fort William to Gairlochy	11.5 miles
DAY 69	Gairlochy to Great Glen Water Park	14 miles
DAY 70	Great Glen Water Park to Invermoriston	19 miles
DAY 71	Invermoriston to Drumnadrochit	15 miles
DAY 72	Drumnadrochit to Inverness	21 miles

Terrain

At last, the Highlands. Some rough walking by Loch Lomond, on Rannoch Moor, and extremely strenuous, hard walking up Ben Nevis. Thereafter followed by some level strolling by the Caledonian Canal, and, if the high route is chosen, more toughish walking high above Loch Ness.

DAY 59 – *Milngavie to Drymen*

Finally, we could say we had reached the Highlands. This is where the beginning of the end begins!! In front of us is one of Britain's most beautiful lochs, along whose 'bonny, bonny banks' we will wander, whilst later on we will climb Britain's highest mountain and walk beside our country's largest body of fresh water, Loch Ness. Most of that excitement is yet to come, though, since the scenery on the walk to Drymen is merely the suggestion of the Highlands at this stage.

For once, on this walk, we encountered other walkers. As soon as we got to Milngavie we came across people with even bigger rucksacks than ours, also embarking on the famous West Highland Way. Strangely, given that this section of the walk was possibly the wildest and most remote of the whole trip, the section from Milngavie to Inverness was when we had to share the paths with others. We met some great people, but we would still have preferred it to be just us, in splendid isolation, as we had experienced for the past 60 days!

Fungi in Mugdock Wood, north of Milngavie

On the West Highland Way at
Mugdock Wood, north of Milngavie

We were still, however, unbelievably fortunate in the weather. The woods leading out of Milngavie were scented with that rich, earthy, damp and fruity odour that can only be autumn, but the air was warm; the sun was trying to pierce the mists; swallows and swifts still swooped across the sky. Beside the path blackberries rambled in profusion, and everywhere, on tree stumps and sprouting from the humus, fungi of all shapes and colours pronounced the season.

At a coffee stop Bob revealed an early birthday present – a second flask filled with hot coffee. We had already drunk the first flaskful, so this was a real treat. Only people who have walked miles in the outdoors believing there is only cold water to drink will understand just how much of a pleasure this was.

For the first time in weeks we felt free again. Life had been difficult at home with my Mum falling, and in and out of hospital, and back home our landlord had threatened to raise our rent by an unsustainable £250 a month, but once back on the walk our troubles faded away. I know of no better cure for sadness or anxiety or stress than putting on a rucksack and walking long distances. It puts everything into perspective.

DAY 60 – *Drymen to Rowardennan*

It was a typically autumnal morning as we reached a viewpoint over Loch Lomond. Spiders webs, festooning every blade of grass and twig, were transformed into bejewelled veils draped elegantly across the earth. There

must be a lot of spiders though! A red squirrel darted across the path as we left the woods and headed steeply up the slopes of Conic Hill, famous (to some) for being directly on the Highland Boundary Fault. Fortunately it's not like the San Andreas Fault, though I suppose there are still little tremors from time to time. The descent is very steep and hard on the knees in parts. Two lads passed us on mountain bikes and very nearly came a cropper on one particularly steep bit.

Balmaha was a bit of a shock as it was packed with people. Coaches filled the car park and multi-cultural crowds wandered around,

Views of Loch Lomond: from Balmaha (above), and looking north towards the Highlands (right)

feeding the ducks. We nevertheless stopped for a coffee on spotting a suitable bench (not to be ignored, good benches), when a large group of Indian tourists piled down to the water's edge and frantically snapped pictures of said ducks. Their tour guide, wearing the obligatory kilt, looked harried, cross and slightly lunatic, which was confirmed when he disappeared behind a bush and proceeded to play the bagpipes badly, torturing *The Skye Boat Song* for his bemused clients. It's a funny old world.

It was quite a relief to get back out into the golden woods and some peace.

DAY 61 – *Rowardennan to Inverarnan*

Rowardennan is perfectly placed for stunning views along Loch Lomond to the mountains beyond. On a cool but sunny morning the route looked enticing but Bob was suffering from a nasty rash on his lower back (wearers of rucksacks in hot weather will be aware of this phenomenon), he announced he also thought he had a sprained wrist, and I had a painful mouth ulcer!

Onwards and upwards though, and the scenery compensated for everything. The lower route along the loch was closed, though I believe it is open again now, so instead we took the forestry road that seemed to climb, and climb, and climb. It was like being in the Alps only when we reached the top we were at something like 500, not 5,000 feet. As the sun came out the views north were outstanding, gentle puffs of white cloud drifting serenely over the crags and corries of the mountains.

It was on this stretch that we met several groups of walkers who were to become regular companions along the way, passing and being passed by us over the next few days. Without knowing their names they became familiar to us as, variously, Blondie (a Scottish girl with blue streaks in her hair); the Lads (one of whom declared *tha hull kneckered us* – translation being: *that hill was*

Left: Looking back south down Loch Lomond from above Ardleish

rather tiring. There was the Dutch Couple (he constantly walked about 50 yards in front of her – did they not like each other?); and the Swiss Chard Metronome (Swiss, steady, regular-paced) who made out with Blondie in the end.

Fortunately none of the above were walking past when I found a little beach beside the crystal-clear loch water and, unable to resist, discarded all clothes and went for a swim. It is one of the great memories of the walk, so perfect was that moment. Dried in the warm sun, we continued on the way past the very busy Inversnaid (a road comes in from the east) and onto the most difficult section of the whole way.

Make no mistake, this is not an easy stroll beside the loch. From Inversnaid onwards, the route becomes narrow, twisting over crags, rocks, tree roots, up little climbs where hands are needed, and down again, only to repeat the whole thing. It's horrible. Our speed dropped to a ridiculous pace and it was hell on knees, ankles, calves and thighs.

On the plus side, the views were increasingly beautiful and the trees were lovely, but it went on forever and at the end my legs felt like jelly. One compensation towards the end was three large red deer right beside a stile and totally unconcerned by us. As we had brushed through tall bracken I was worried about ticks and on arrival at Inverarnan the first job was to check each other thoroughly for the nasty little beasts. Bob had quite a large one clambering about on his underpants! Seriously though, be aware of these pests. They can carry Lyme disease and you may well become infected if they latch onto you and start sucking your blood.

Beinglas Farm was a haven after such a hard day. Our room was warm and comfortable, there was a huge open fire burning in a hearth outside, and they served us great fish and chips and chocolate fudge cake. Perfect.

Above right: Our swimming spot on Loch Lomond
Right: A red deer hind close to the loch

131

Remnants of the Old Caledonian Forest, Glen Falloch.

DAY 62 – *Inverarnan to Tyndrum*

The road on the opposite side of Glen Falloch was busy with motorbikes on the gloriously sunny Sunday morning as we climbed away from Loch Lomond towards Crianlarich, but other than that, the day was perfect. On the slopes above us the remnants of the old Caledonian pine forest cast umbrella shadows over the graceful, golden silver birches and bushy willows. Streams flowing off the hill were cold and clear, strewn with the fallen autumn leaves; rowan berries, luscious ruby red, dangled enticingly over soft carpets of moss. It was one of the most exquisite mornings I have ever experienced.

High above Crianlarich we sat beside an icy stream to dabble our feet and search for gold. Yes, there *is* gold in them thar hills! There is actually an operational gold mine at Cononish near Tyndrum and people still come to the area to try their luck at panning for gold. We didn't find any.

Just outside Tyndrum you cross the battle site of Dalrigh (King's Field, in Gaelic), where Robert the Bruce was defeated by the MacDougalls and apparently threw his weapons into a small loch during his retreat. Walking past Lochan nan Arm, you pass a bench inscribed with the legend of the lost sword. It's all very romantic.

Less so is the bare patch of ground just beyond which was poisoned by lead smelting and where nothing will now grow. Imagine what it did to the workers.

Tyndrum was awful. Even in winter when we have driven through in the car, there tend to be people about, but on a sunny Sunday the place was heaving with people and motorbikes. Our hotel room was dark and dingy, but at least clean and at the rear of the building, so away from the thronging hordes.

St Fillan's Priory South of Tyndrum

The River Falloch at Derrydaroch

Day 63 – *Tyndrum to Inveroran*

This was a truly exciting day for us. So many times we have driven the wonderfully scenic road up out of Tyndrum, past the magnificent swooping slopes of Beinn Dorain and up to Bridge of Orchy, and now we were going to walk it. I had prayed that this day would be fine, and, like nearly all of them had been, it was.

Interestingly, the Tyndrum graveyard, opened (is that the right word?) in 2005, only had one grave in it. Bob said that either everyone here lived a very long time, or no one lived here! [We have passed it since and it now has two.]

The route takes you beside the railway along most of the glen up to Bridge of Orchy, so there was much excitement and childish waving when a train passed by, though we didn't see the Jacobite steam train.

Wisps of cloud capped Beinn Dorain's summit and drifted down its steep, riven flanks towards the glen below, before the wind picked up and the sun came out to lift the colours and the clouds.

Being plagued by a wasp at Bridge of Orchy station we decided not to have a break there but instead sat by the river watching trout leap out of the water.

On the way to Inveroran we passed a warning sign saying "That which burns never returns", which is true of the UK but made me think of Australia where fire is often an essential part of a plant's life cycle. Oddly enough when we reached the hotel there were four Australians staying, two of whom, believe it or not, were called Bruce. The hotel held a lot of memories for me as I remember dancing a jig in the courtyard one New Year's Eve years ago!

Looking up the valley of the Allt Kinglass (Gleann Achadh-Innis Chailein) near Auch with Beinn a Chasteil shrouded in cloud on the right

DAY 64 – *Inveroran to Kingshouse*

We awoke to a stunning dawn of pink mists and drifting clouds, forecasting another sunny day. The route climbs steadily out of the glen using a drovers' road designed by our old friend of Pontcysllyte aquaduct fame, Thomas Telford. That man certainly got about! Bob commented that the canny Scots must have sold Telford all their pointed stones for his road, as the track was very rough and uncomfortable to walk in parts!

The higher the route climbed, the more impressive the views became, mist drifting across the mountains, bare, windswept moors offering up a wild, wide view. Despite the fact that we saw more people on the West Highland Way than on the rest of our walk put together, there is no doubt that crossing the Black Mount, with magnificent Coire Ba to your left and the remote wet expanse of Rannoch Moor stretching to infinity to your right, is one of the wildest feelings you will have on the walk. Whatever the weather, these are miles to savour.

At Ba Bridge the river tumbles down over the rocks beneath birch and rowan trees, whilst upstream at its source the great serrated ridges of the Munros stand silent and brooding. These rocks have been here long before man existed, they have watched armies march past them, eagles nest in their cliffs, the world turns around them but still they stand, eternal, solid, watching. I feel a power, a strength from the mountains, a oneness with them. At Ba Bridge I felt an urge to strike out upriver and be absorbed into the mountains. It is that powerful.

Dawn over the Mam Carraigh from Inveroran

Glencoe Mountain Café will certainly bring you back down to earth with a bump! The whole place lacked atmosphere and decent service but if the chairlift is running and you have time, it may be worth hopping on and getting up to a couple of thousand feet for a spectacular view.

The Kingshouse Hotel can be a bit of a mixed bag, but given that there is little other accommodation in the area, you probably have to take it or leave it. Our room was warm, with a spectacular view of Buachaille Etive Mor, but supper in the bar was a bit grim with sticky tables and the surliest bartender we have ever encountered.

Looking towards Stob a Choire Odhair from the West Highland Way south of Ba Bridge

DAY 65 – *Kingshouse to Kinlochleven*

It was good to leave Kingshouse behind us in the morning with the sun casting shafts onto the peaks and the mists rising over the river.

On this day I run out of superlatives to describe what we saw. Sunlight, drifting shadow, gullied, riven cliffs and bare, weathered rock, red deer grazing on the slopes. Utterly magnificent. Perhaps my photographs will speak for me instead.

As we topped the rise above the Devil's Staircase out of Glencoe, things became, if possible, even more spectacular. It was breathtaking. Before us lay the whole range of the Mamores, peak after peak, rolling like waves into the distance; scree and corries and ridges adorned with a succession of misty rainbows. I have rarely seen anything finer. Memories came flooding back, of once camping out alone in that vastness, and waking in the midst of an icy, moonlit night, to find my tent surrounded by deer.

Two American walkers asked us if they could go along the Aonach Eagach ridge then down into Kinlochleven. We informed them that the ridge required nerves of steel and a rope in parts, and I think that discouraged them sufficiently, but at least we couldn't be blamed if they had a go!

As you approach Kinlochleven you are accompanied by massive hydro-electric pipes carrying the water downhill to the generators. In the quiet you can hear the rumble of the water inside. Unfortunately Kinlochleven, whilst

Buachaille Etive Mor, near Kingshouse

Above: The River Ba at Ba Bridge
Right: Looking back to Buachaille Etive Mor and the River Coupall from the Devil's Staircase

142

Black Rock Cottage with Buachaille Etive Mor behind

beautifully situated, is not a pretty town. It owed its existence to the aluminium smelter which is now closed, and today tourism is its main purpose. The village houses the National Ice Climbing Centre, and of course the West Highland Way brings thousands of visitors, so regeneration and improvement is ongoing and no doubt in the near future Kinlochleven will be a superb place to visit.

Day 66 – *Kinlochleven to Fort William*

Our first rainy day for weeks! Climbing steeply out of Kinlochleven, we reached the narrow pass of the Lairigmor, which on a sunny day is impressive but on a cold, wet, windy morning is a bit of a slog! It is several miles of rough track high up between the ridges, the Mamores looming above to your right (when you can see them), until eventually the track turns north to head to Fort William. On a sunny day we would have been good and followed the West Highland Way across Nevis Forest into Glen Nevis, but we were soaked, the rain was stingingly cold in our faces, and at Blar a Chaorainn a small road appears that leads you directly down into the town. We took it!!

A wet day above Kinlochleven

Day 67 – *Ben Nevis*

A scary, scary day! There is no reason why Ben Nevis makes me so afraid, but I had been dreading climbing it for weeks, and this was the day. We had once contemplated climbing Snowdon and Scafell as part of the walk, doing the three highest peaks on the UK mainland, but the diversion from our route would have been too great. No excuse not to climb the Ben though! Once we started, the fear vanished. For a start, we were not alone, with many other people climbing alongside us. Secondly, the path is obvious and cannot be mistaken, though I appreciate that in snow this may be different, and thirdly, the sun was out and visibility good except for the very top of the mountain. Graceful shafts of sunlight pierced the clouds and illuminated the glens and peaks around us as we climbed, providing distraction from the hard slog up. In a quiet moment we could hear stags roaring below us in the glen. It's a thrilling, wild, sound and a reminder of the wonders these mountains hold.

Do not be deceived, this is a hard day. You will cover some 15 miles and climb nearly 4,600 feet and if your legs aren't aching and shaky at the end of that, you're a better person than me!

The top is a different world. On the very occasional day when it is clear and there isn't a howling gale it must be spectacular, but on our visit we entered cloud, came across a fierce, icy wind and hail showers. No doubt hardier folk will scoff at us for taking the so-called tourist route, insisting that the Ben should only be climbed and appreciated from the North Face or via the Carn Mor Dearg Arete, and they are probably right, but

Am Bodach and The Mamores from the top of the Devil's Staircase above Kinlochleven

nevertheless it still felt like a huge achievement. We peered down Gardy Loo Gully which is only about 10 steps away from the main path, and it was a sheer, terrifyingly long way down.

As the sun was setting, hordes of people passed us, going up. These were groups doing the Three Peaks Challenge, still with Scafell and Snowdon to come. Some looked very fresh and keen whilst others were already, only half a mile up the path, looking very doubtful. One lad asked us if that was the top he could see, but unfortunately for him it was nowhere near. We thought about them all for the rest of the night, slogging up and down, seeing nothing, then slumping in sleep until they had to do it again in the Lake District. Each to their own.

Looking up Glen Nevis from the slopes of Ben Nevis

Fort William

A day off! We had a wonderful, restful day, strolling about, snoozing, checking the details for our onward journey, relaxing. Fort William looked after us well.

DAY 68 – *Fort William to Gairlochy*

Today you start the Great Glen Way which will lead you north to Inverness and so much nearer your ultimate goal. The walking is some of the easiest you will have done on the whole journey, often beside the pretty Caledonian Canal (Thomas Telford again) or along quiet lanes and tracks beside the various lochs along the Great Glen.

Above: Corpach and Loch Linnhe from Ben Nevis
Below: On the summit of Ben Nevis

Neptune's Staircase at Banavie is the longest set of canal locks in Britain, lifting boats about 60 feet. It's an impressive sight, and from the top, on a clear day, the views back towards Ben Nevis and the Grey Corries are spectacular. Unfortunately we had a 'dreich' day, one of those highland days when the mist is down and the rain drips on your waterproofs with a dreadful monotony. We were lucky, however, that by the evening the weather cleared and at our B&B just outside Gairlochy we could wander up the

hill to the wonderful Commando Memorial above Spean Bridge, and enjoy the views of the mountains that we had been missing all day. The memorial was opened in 1952 as a tribute to the Commandos who trained in the area during the Second World War. There is a wonderful statue and a Garden of Remembrance, and if you can visit in the evening as we did, when the tourists have gone home, it is a very moving experience.

DAY 69 – *Gairlochy to Great Glen Water Park*

After yesterday's rain, this day dawned pure, clear and clean, the sun sparkling on Loch Lochy and lighting the sharp gullies of the Ben's North Face, where in some places the snow still lingered. The morning was so warm, and the loch so beautiful, fringed with autumnal beeches, that I was tempted to swim again, but we had a deadline to meet on this day as we needed to catch a bus back to Spean Bridge to our accommodation, there being none at North Laggan, so I resisted the temptation and simply savoured the joy of being alive on such a stunning highland morning.

The Commando Memorial, Spean Bridge

Along the path we came across a little fairy shrine where there were presents of pretty stones and berries left by passers-by for the fairies. Feeling fairly silly but nonetheless involved in the magic, I left my own little gift for the spirits. And indeed, the forest we then entered was a perfect home for elves and sprites. Sunlight filtered through tall dark trees onto a mossy blanket of lichens and ferns, criss-crossed with delightful streams, while above our heads birds flitted and chirped in the quiet of the canopy.

Back out beside the loch Bob saw something huge jump out of the water and splash back in. Perhaps Nessie had moved south?

All along the way we came across more information about the Commandos, on interesting information boards. One part of the training was to do speed marches of increasing lengths in reducing times, beginning with 7 miles in 70 minutes. For us, plodding along even with our relatively light packs, that sounded impossible.

At a stop for a paddle in a waterfall we came across two guys who went on to share the way with us right into Inverness. One was always in front and always talking, the other behind and silent so Bob nicknamed them rather rudely, 'One man and his dog'. We saw no one else on the Great Glen Way so mostly we were back in our own empty space, just saying hello occasionally as we passed the pair or they passed us.

Forest path on the shores of Loch Lochy

DAY 70 – *Great Glen Water Park to Invermoriston*

This was my birthday and should have been a great day but I then received a message that my Mum was in hospital with a terrible pain in her head and inability to move. There was no way we could get back to her quickly so there was little alternative but to keep walking until we got more information and arrived somewhere we could get a train home. The next few miles were simply a mist of tears and guilt and fear, but I am sure that under normal circumstances the walk along the shores of Loch Oich to Aberchalder would be utterly delightful.

Fortunately later in the day I managed to speak to my Mum who was feeling much better and told us not to worry. So we decided to wait and see what news the next day brought, and continued on to Fort Augustus. What a shock we got there! The little town was heaving with people to such an extent it was barely possible to walk on the pavement. We hurriedly left.

At Fort Augustus a choice has to be made. Here the Great Glen Way has two possible routes, the low and high versions. The high version had opened just a few weeks before we walked it and this was the option we chose since it gets you out above the trees with expansive views north and south down the glen. I can recommend it but do be aware that there are some extremely steep climbs and descents. Not good if you have bad knees!

What the high route does give you is a sense of just how big Loch Ness is. Driving along it you zip past and don't get a sense of the scale, but looking down on it filling the width of the glen, you appreciate the mass of water that is down there. I looked up the statistics: 800 feet deep, 23 miles long, holding 263,000 million cubic feet of water, more than all the lakes in England and Wales combined! And of course, then there is Nessie…

The head of Nessie, most famous of local residents

DAY 71 – *Invermoriston to Drumnadrochit*

On this day we decided to combine parts of the high and low routes, to get the best of both worlds and avoid some of the steepest climbing, though even the low route ascends to over a thousand feet, giving the same stunning views down the glen and across it to the remote wildness of the Monadhliath Mountains to the east. Once again the sun shone on attractive forests brightened with gorse, broom and birch, tall pines clinging to sheer rock above us. In the shadows great heaps of wood ant nests reminded us of the miniature life that goes on unnoticed as we humans tramp along.

The good news today from my sister was that my Mum was much improved. After talking to Mum who sounded more like her old self, we decided to continue to Inverness to decide there whether to return home or not.

We were already settled at table for dinner when 'One man and his dog' arrived at 8.30pm, looking totally shattered. They had stopped the previous day at Fort Augustus and therefore had an immensely long walk to Drumnadrochit, taking the high route. They looked most surprised to see us lounging at our ease, but we had done the hard work the day before!

Looking east across Loch Ness from the Great Glen Way 'High Route' near Bunloit

DAY 72 – *Drumnadrochit to Inverness*

This is not a terribly hard day, but it is a long one, over 21 miles into the centre of Inverness, so gird up your loins and get cracking early.

You may have noticed that since Glasgow I have not mentioned blisters once. Unaccountably, from Glasgow onwards my feet remained clear of soreness and blisters, all the way to John O'Groats. It immeasurably increased the amount of pleasure I took from the walk, to be pain-free every day!

Drumnadrochit is another of those tourist-magnet places that we were happy to leave. Throngs of Japanese tourists were taking photographs of everything whilst being serenaded (if that is the right word) by the ubiquitous bagpipes. Nessieland Castle Monster Centre has such delights as mini golf and a model railway: enough said. Urquhart Castle, on the promontory just south of Drumnadrochit, is impossibly picturesque, and worth a visit if you can avoid the thousands of other people doing the same.

Once again the route climbed steeply up into forests where there were some interesting boards telling the story of Canadian lumberjacks working the forest during World War II. About 2,000 men came over, and were called 'Newfies' as mostly they came from Newfoundland. Needless to say, many of them met and married bonny Scottish lasses and never went home.

Close to Abriachan we began to see roughly-painted wooden signs enticing us to drink Bovril, proper tea, or hot chocolate. It was a wonderful marketing ploy as gradually the signs and suggestions increased until we were practically salivating at the thought of a nice cosy sit-down in a lovely café. Well, it wasn't quite what we had expected. Turning just a little off the route we passed through grounds where pigs were rooting happily and then came upon a series of huts that looked half-built, where dogs barked and more pigs rooted. Unsure, we were about to

Urquhart Castle, Drumnadrochit

154

turn back when we were warmly invited in by the patroness. 'In' is not actually the right word as we were offered rickety plastic chairs underneath an awning, through which an icy wind blew. The hand-written menu specialized in 'freshly grounded coffee'. Off to our left some cages held what looked like wolves, so thereafter the place was referred to by us as Wolf Creek. It was one of the quirkiest and oddest places we encountered, but the Bovril was good.

Back en route, we began to glimpse views of Ben Wyvis and the mountains of the north, a thrilling sight, urging us on, northwards, to the finish.....

And finally we arrived in Inverness, walking along the Caledonian Canal and the River Ness into the sunny, pretty riverside centre of our last city. Looking out over the river from our apartment, incredible lenticular clouds were mysteriously lit by the setting sun. It felt as if we truly had arrived in a strange, unknown land.

On the following day we heard more news about Mum and decided that we needed to go home. More tears and guilt ensued, but we knew we would return, we were so close now...

Lenticular clouds over Inverness

On reflection

Joy, wonder, anticipation, pride and some sadness were the main emotions on this section. We were graced throughout with the most perfect autumn weather which lifted the Highlands to an even greater level of beauty. It was a joy to walk through such glories.

And by the time we reached Inverness we had moved from somewhere in the south to being what felt like nearly there… The achievement of a dream: just one more section of the walk to go.

Sadness came because I was worried and frightened for my Mum, and terribly torn between my love for her and my desire not to ruin the walk for my beloved Bob. He, of course, stood behind me whatever my decision and was my rock throughout.

We went home, but couldn't wait to come back.

Inverness and the north bank of the river

157

Ackergill Links at Sinclair's Bay, north of Wick

STAGE 7
9 Days – 137 miles

The Last Leg
Inverness to John O'Groats

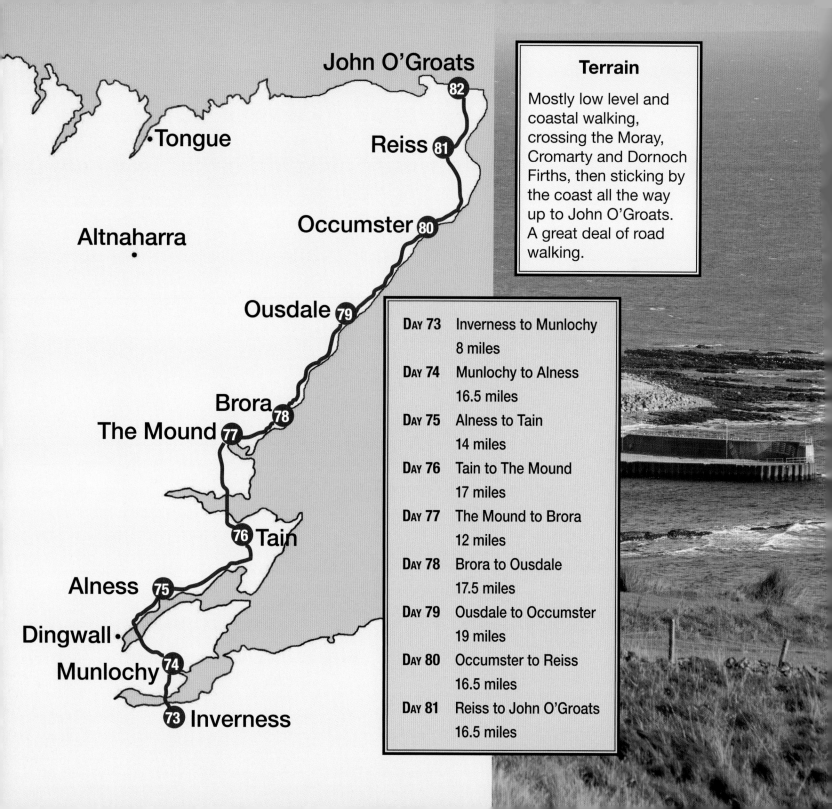

John O'Groats **82**

Reiss **81**

•Tongue

Occumster **80**

Altnaharra
.

Ousdale **79**

Brora **78**

The Mound **77**

Tain **76**

Alness **75**

Dingwall •

Munlochy **74**

73 Inverness

Terrain

Mostly low level and coastal walking, crossing the Moray, Cromarty and Dornoch Firths, then sticking by the coast all the way up to John O'Groats. A great deal of road walking.

DAY 73	Inverness to Munlochy	8 miles
DAY 74	Munlochy to Alness	16.5 miles
DAY 75	Alness to Tain	14 miles
DAY 76	Tain to The Mound	17 miles
DAY 77	The Mound to Brora	12 miles
DAY 78	Brora to Ousdale	17.5 miles
DAY 79	Ousdale to Occumster	19 miles
DAY 80	Occumster to Reiss	16.5 miles
DAY 81	Reiss to John O'Groats	16.5 miles

DAY 73 – *Inverness to Munlochy*

Having been at home with my Mum for two weeks and with her heartfelt blessing, we returned to Inverness in mid October. The start was hard though. Neither of us felt 'in the groove', I had a horrible cold and cough I couldn't shake off, my ankles hurt, legs ached and the traffic as we walked out of Inverness was horrible!

Once beyond the Kessock Bridge, though, we began to relax a little. Bob's idea was that we would walk to the right rather than the left at the end of the bridge and find our way across Ord Hill. Please note: this is NOT recommended! We ended up very close to the shore, with cliffs to our left, and the tide coming in rather rapidly. At one point there was about two yards between the water and the cliff.

We did hope to at least catch a glimpse of the Moray Firth dolphins, but no luck. There were great views of the bridge though. When we climbed up onto Ord Hill, there was no path. We struggled about through bracken for a while during which I got badly bitten on my calf, then reluctantly returned to the scary shore and battled our way along until we came to Kilmuir where there was, finally, some good solid tarmac. Not a good start! You are much better, I think, to turn left at the end of the bridge and follow the cycle track into North Kessock and thence to Drumsmittal.

Things did improve after that. The Black Isle is fairly flat and unremarkable but easy walking, often through field after field of Christmas trees, all tagged and priced ready, at that time of year, for the Christmas market.

Above: country road near Alness

Left: Kessock Bridge, Inverness

161

The Moray Firth from The Black Isle

DAY 74 – *Munlochy to Alness*

A pastoral sort of day, quiet and peaceful, with nothing remarkable except for the approach to the crossing of the Cromarty Firth on the causeway, when we saw our first road sign for John O'Groats, 109 miles away. Only 109 miles to go! My heart thumped a little with excited anticipation.

The crossing and subsequent road on the other side were no fun at all. Whilst there was a footpath on the causeway it was dangerously narrow and as lorries thundered past, not at all pleasant. It was worse on the other side as we had to walk along a very uneven verge which really hurt my ankles so I rather foolishly decided to walk on the road. This was OK until a mad driver in a Volkswagen decided to overtake and missed me by inches. After that I put up with the verge.

Oblivious of the traffic, several dozen seals lounged on the shore and above our heads geese flew noisily past in various V formations, heading south for the winter. An information board told us these were Icelandic Greylag Geese, for whom the Cromarty Firth is a popular overwintering spot. The stubble fields on the backroads off the A9 were smothered in geese.

The Firth is a parking spot for unused oil rigs, awaiting either a return to service or scrapping, and they looked odd as they appear out of the mist beyond the green, goose-grazed fields.

Alness where we stayed the night was a little grim. We decided therefore to have tea in our room and I have to say here, if I have not said it before, how much my wonderful Bob looked after me throughout our walk. He did most of the washing, sandwich making and cooking on the nights we didn't eat out and he generally made delicious food with very few resources. On this night he presented me with soup, bread, salami, oatcakes with cheese and tomato, followed by chocolate pot with grapes. My darling Bob, I salute you.

Day 75 – *Alness to Tain*

This felt like a very easy day, though we covered 14 miles. The sun shone yet again, we took a tiny, quiet road lined with birch, larch and hips in all their autumn colours, we lounged around on a grassy bank drinking coffee, and arrived into Tain at the luxuriously early time of 3pm. Deciding that we would eat in again, we found, to our delight and surprise, a Tesco store and then proceeded to our B&B in the hope of an early entry and a nice relaxing evening. No such luck. The B&B informed us, when we rang, that entry was impossible before 4pm. Ten minutes later he rang to say that he had been trying to ring me all day (a lie, my phone had a signal all day), and

Redundant oil rigs parked in the Cromarty Firth

Loch Fleet at The Mound, south of Golspie

that his wife's mother was ill so they had to go out and couldn't accommodate us at all. Fortunately we found a little B&B just opposite and stayed there. Interestingly we could see our original venue and no-one left but several cars arrived. Could he possibly have double booked, we wondered??

It didn't matter, in the end. Our alternative B&B was run by a retired gentleman who had been in the Merchant Navy for 40 years and loved travelling the world until the advent of container ships meant that the turnaround in the dock was so rapid he never got the chance to go ashore and explore. We felt rather sad for him.

A repeat of yesterday! Warm sun, uneventful, pastoral lanes, and a mad crossing of, this time, the Dornoch Firth. As with the Cromarty Firth, the causeway walk across the water had narrow footways and totally crazy drivers, but once across we followed the quiet little coast road leading into Dornoch, which is one of the prettiest and most delightful small towns in Scotland. To me, Dornoch has just about everything (except, of course, Mediterranean sunshine, which would be nice). There is the wonderful, clean sandy beach which naturally required me to paddle while Bob looked on, bored; the wonderful links golf course which apparently has recently been voted 5th best in the world (!) and the lovely stone town, centred around the exquisite little 13th century cathedral. It's perfect.

We strolled along the coast towards Embo, which consisted mostly of caravans belonging to *Grannie's Heilan Hame* holiday park. It was tidy and pleasant, beautifully situated on the shore, but surely they could have thought of a less cringe-making name?

Greylags and gulls at Loch Fleet, The Mound

Loch Fleet, a mile or so further on, is a tidal basin and nature reserve, with a breeding population of ospreys, though we were too late in the year to see them. There were however lots of other birds, waders, ducks and of course the geese again, so it was a refreshing and pleasurable walk along the shore until we encountered the nasty A9 again to cross The Mound. Guess what? The bridge across the joining point of Loch and River Fleet was designed by - yep, Thomas Telford.

It's an interesting spot as Telford's old bridge, now no longer in use, has clever sluice gates that stop the sea water travelling up-river but allow the river water out, leaving a fresh water lagoon on the landward side that is also a nature reserve.

Back in Dornoch as the sun was setting the limpid sky blackened with wave after wave of geese flying over, all calling, hauntingly wild. It was quite something. To celebrate we decided to splash out and thus ate like kings at the Royal Dornoch Golf Hotel. I remarked in my notes that the sticky toffee pudding was the best ever (in capital letters) so it must have been really special but I confess I can't bring it to mind now.

Dunrobin Castle, Golspie,
Seat of the Duke of Sutherland

Seals in the bay near Brora

DAY 77 – *The Mound to Brora*

The first mile or so we had to follow the A9 but as it was early Sunday morning, for once the road was bearable and not too dangerous. We were soon able to turn off towards Balblair Wood and the next links golf course on the south side of Golspie. We had started out in pouring rain but by mid-morning our usual luck had returned and we were blessed again with warm sunshine as we sat overlooking the sea for our morning coffee.

Then onwards, and we came across the fairytale Dunrobin Castle, seat of the Dukes of Sutherland. One of the largest and oldest continuously inhabited castles, with 189 rooms, the castle dates back to the 1300s, though it was remodelled in 1854 by the architect for the Houses of Parliament, Sir Charles Barry. It is out of place in such a windswept and remote location, but nevertheless manages to be utterly beautiful.

DAY 78 – *Brora to Ousdale*

Having had a swim in the pool and a lounge in the Jacuzzi at last night's luxurious hotel in Brora we should have been remarkably refreshed when setting out, but I for one was still feeling the effects of my cold and a poor night's sleep, so my legs were a bit reluctant to get going. The hotel in Brora was lovely however, a beautiful old building designed in 1913 by a proponent of the Arts and Crafts style, with a lovely old snooker room and great wooden staircases and panelled rooms. Like many other hotels in this area, it sits rather oddly amongst houses in the centre of Brora. The towns and villages along this far north-east coast we found to be peculiar little places, almost forgotten by time, quiet and often neglected, except for the traffic passing through on the A9, though even that was steadily diminishing as we proceeded further north.

Our first mile or so was again alongside yet another beautiful links course. Clearly, this is a prime area to visit if you happen to be a keen golfer. I am very poor at it, but I can see the appeal of these wonderful rolling greens and fairways, and they make for great walking!

Unfortunately the A9 is not so good for a pedestrian. Thankfully the traffic was reducing but when lorries or buses passed, there was very little room to get out of the way. And there really is no alternative, the only other choice being to turn inland at The Mound and walk to the north coast at Tongue, then turn east from there. We will do that next time, just for a change.

After Helmsdale, another oddly sad little town with a pretty harbour, we climbed steeply up to our hotel at Navidale, enjoying the wonderful, sunny views over the North Sea and out to the many oil rigs standing like leviathans over the deep. As it was only just after lunch, Bob suggested we walk further that afternoon, then to Lybster and Wick on the following days, and thus arrive at John O'Groats a day early. Brilliant! We were still walking the A9 but this time with a wider grassy verge and cycleway. This part of the road follows the heads of many 'geos', clefts in the sea cliffs caused by wave erosion along fault lines, so there was quite a bit of winding in and out!

The rainbow after Hurricane Gonzalo had passed through

At Ousdale we had arranged for a taxi to take us back to our hotel at Navidale. You will find that these are the sort of arrangements that you need to make, not just in the far north, but in all the remote areas that you walk through. It makes for an interesting organizational challenge and you need to be ready to change plans!

Our hotel was a peaceful, old fashioned retreat, with a four poster bed, wonderful sea views, coal fires burning in bar and restaurant, and great food. I could imagine staying there for several days, completely relaxing and forgetting that the world outside existed.

DAY 79 – *Ousdale to Occumster*

The weather forecasters had been warning of a hurricane reaching Scotland – and it did. Northern Scotland had winds gusting up to 100mph and lashings of rain. And we walked through it all. At times the only way to be safe was to cling to each other and turn our backs, waiting for the pounding air to pass over us. Walking into the wind was possible only by bending double. For once we were thankful for the weight in our rucksacks since at times it stopped us being blown into the road. Fortunately many motorists seemed to have heeded warnings not to travel, so for once the A9 was exceedingly quiet.

At Badbea, perched on the bleak cliff, are the sad remains of a clearance village. The people were forced off their fertile crofts inland and Badbea was their only alternative, but the life was so hard that when even herring fishing died out, so did the settlement. The last resident left the village in 1911, whilst others had long before departed, many emigrating to the new worlds of Australia, and New Zealand.

After we left the pretty little village of Berriedale nestled in a hollow, the wind got even worse as we climbed steeply onto the tops of the cliffs. The noise of the wind was so loud we had to shout to be heard, as we staggered onwards.

At Dunbeath a bus shelter became a total haven for half an hour as we sheltered eating our lunch. It even had a proper bench to sit on instead of those awful sloping plastic bits you find in modern shelters these days. What use are they to anyone? Strange how usually overlooked objects like a bus shelter can be wonderful things when walking through a hurricane.

From the sublime (our hotel last night) to the ridiculous…. our B&B at Occumster was most odd. We shared, unwillingly, in the life of the house, eating our evening meal beside a covered snooker table under which were piles of games and papers, whilst the young son played, loudly, at shooting people on his Xbox. Our room was cold, dusty, and unfinished, with dowdy pictures propped up against the wall. One of the few places on the walk we would not return to!

DAY 80 – *Occumster to Reiss*

A grey, grey, day. The wind had died, but it rained steadily, all day. The sea was grey, the sky was grey, even the houses were grey. Why on earth, we wondered, do the people up here not paint their houses white, or yellow, or pink: anything except grey?

We had hoped to walk off-road along the coast for much of the way but couldn't find the track down to the cliffs beyond Ulbster and as the weather was so miserable we decided instead just to press on along the road and get there. At Thrumster we found a little heritage railway centre with a bench and a canopy where we sat out of the rain for a while, but to be honest it was a miserable afternoon's walk into Wick along a straight, boring road. We had said goodbye, finally, to the A9 just before Lybster so we were now on the A99, but it made little difference, it was still a busy road.

Wick, veiled in the distance by sweeping curtains of rain, looked as grey as everywhere else. But at least it was a proper town! I'm sure in sunshine it may look a little better, and it does have some interesting things to see, like the shortest street in the world at just 6 feet long, a proud history stretching back to the Vikings and was once the busiest fishing port in

Below left: Ebenezer Place, Wick, the world's shortest street
Below right: Looking north from Dunbeath

Britain when the herring fishing was at its height. And surprise, surprise, the town's harbour was improved by Mr Thomas Telford.

At Wick there is a choice. You can walk out to the coast at Staxigoe and follow the headland around to Ackergill, or you can do as we did and cut the corner off by continuing on the road. Perhaps, on a sunny day, we might have chosen the longer route, but then again, maybe not. We were about 16 miles from John O'Groats and the urge to finish had become overwhelming. After so many miles and days, the finish line was compelling, drawing us onwards by the shortest and quickest route. I admire anyone who by this stage still has the desire to take an unnecessary detour.

Keiss Castle and Sinclair's Bay north of Wick

We therefore walked through Wick and out to the crossroads at Reiss, then caught a bus back into town, stopping off at Tesco on the way. Our B&B was a haven: warm, spotlessly clean, perfect. Unfortunately that evening I received an email from my publishers that made me think they were not going to be able to publish my first book on the Forest of Bowland, and I was ridiculously, utterly, out of control tearful. Poor Bob could do nothing with me.

DAY 81 – *Reiss to John O'Groats*

Oh my goodness, the last day. I awoke with massive anxiety, still worrying about my book but also almost afraid of reaching John O'Groats. It had been an obsession for two years: what on earth were we going to feel when we got there? What were we going to obsess about next? We had decided that we would walk the coastal route on this day, so I was anxious about that too, as the map did not actually show any paths between Reiss and Keiss. Bob had read somewhere that we could walk along the beach with no difficulty, though he was slightly worried about crossing the River of Wester which meets the sea halfway along. I dismissed this worry, saying we could just paddle in the sea to get across.

At first, it was wonderful. The sun came out behind us, although in front the sky was black and stormy, brilliant white seagulls whirled against the inky sky, two seals reared up in the water and splashed a welcome. Then we reached the river. As we approached, we could see the brown peat of the river staining the sea far out beyond the beach. On closer inspection the river was frightening: wide, raging, deep, dark brown, tossed with waves as the tide pushed against it. To try and cross the river would have been suicide, and as for wading into the sea, that would have been the end of us too. What to do? We never liked to retrace our steps, and once again we determined that we would not do so in this case. Instead we walked upriver, forded several smaller streams with boots and socks off, struggled across some boggy bits, sneaked across a golf course, staggered over some rough ground, crossed a barbed wire fence, crossed a soaking wet field, and hallelujah, we were back on the road, safe! It seemed appropriate that, on our last day, we should once again have a section of the walk that turned out to be, in our words, epic!

Further along the road we realised that at the far end of the beach, huge yellow pipelines emerged from the sea. As we passed by we noticed that the pipe was moving slowly inland, on rails. It was most impressive. Had we braved the dangers and crossed the river somehow, we would have found ourselves turned back by this pipeline, having to re-ford the river. There would have been some wailing and gnashing of teeth then, I can tell you.

Lobster pots, John O

oats Harbour

Sitting outside the Caithness Broch Centre (closed) we met a man from Leyland who told us proudly that he had just bought the old school next door to where we were sitting, for just £52,000. Bob thought he had been robbed.

The coast here is dotted with old castles, which make for great pictures, but Bob did wonder what their defensive purpose was. He said if he had been a Viking he would have just landed somewhere else and left the inhabitants of the castle alone. Or maybe that was the point.

The Old John O'Groats Hotel
John O'Groats

At Freswick you could walk down to the cliff and along the coast to Duncansby Head, which is the true most north-easterly point of the British mainland, but we had been scared by our experience on the beach (or at least I had) and with the finish compulsion on us again, we stuck to the road. We did later walk out to Duncansby Head and the wonderful stacks, once we had arrived at John O'Groats, as we stayed in the area for several days.

At the top of the long drag up heather-covered Warth Hill our final destination was revealed at last. Down below us, looking out towards the Orkney Islands, was John O'Groats. 2 miles to go. We were going to finish! We strolled down the hill in the sunshine, which miraculously had been our almost constant companion for 90% of our walk, relaxed, content, knowing it was done.

Two cyclists passed us, clearly also having come from Land's End, and sure enough, suddenly we were at the signpost and they were already there, laughing, calling out, 'We beat you!' We took pictures of them and they did the same for us.

There were ordinary people milling about, tourists, but we were alone, with the cyclists, in our own little bubble. Only we knew what this meant. I sobbed in Bob's arms. Why? Relief, joy, sorrow at finishing, pride at the sheer bloody (literally, sometimes) achievement, all those hours and days and weeks spent with the man I adore, crossing the country I love. I find it almost impossible to accurately describe this last day and these final moments.

Bob felt it too and said later it was like walking in a mind fog, a living dream. He says that at that very moment he could see and feel every step of the route we had taken, as if he were flying, at speed, a few feet above the ground, visualising that snaking route all the way back to the far south. That path that took us all the way from the blue sea of Land's End to this wild northern outpost is seared in our imagination forever.

You'll discover, when you too reach John O'Groats, that you'll want to keep on walking – there's no stopping now...

We made it! Bob and Helen at John O'Groats

176

On reflection

We had decided to savour John O'Groats so were booked for a few days in a lovely apartment overlooking the sea. Here we opened an envelope from Bob's son Philip, who had made us a card and a sort of certificate of achievement. I sobbed my heart out again at such kindness and love. (I am an emotional person, you may have gathered this by now.)

There we were, done. How did I, how do I feel? Proud of myself, joyous, strong. Walking from Land's End to John O'Groats is one of the greatest achievements of my life. That I did it in the constant company of my wonderful Bob, the love of my life, just adds to the joy and is something that can never be taken away from us. Was there one thing that defined the walk? No, not one, a multitude. Trying to write them down would result in a complicated mess of verbosity, so here is a short list instead:

1. Sore feet and frayed Achilles tendons

For something like 800 miles I walked with pain. There were times when I woke in the morning in tears, convinced I could walk no further and then, through absolute determination, I would walk 19 miles. On day one, crossing Sennen Cove, sharp jabs of pain shot up my ankles and I prayed that my frayed Achilles tendons would not stop me from completing the walk. I told myself then that I had to walk through the pain and ignore it, which I did for the next 1,000 miles. At some stage on every single day, my ankles hurt. Some may say, how foolish to walk under such circumstances! I say, it taught me that if I want to, I can do anything. I will never forget that lesson. When things seem bleak and hopeless and hard, I remind myself what I can do.

2. Excitement

On every single day of the walk, despite tears and anxiety, I awoke with excitement. To know that you are going to walk through an unknown part of your own marvellous country, to see new places, walk to a town or village you have never visited before... what fun it has been to do that. This was, truly, a voyage of discovery.

3. The B&Bs

All the multifarious places we stayed, across England, Wales and Scotland; some good, some superb, many just ordinary, one or two, poor. Yet each place we stayed we were glad to reach, to shrug off the heavy weights from our backs, unlace boots from sore, tired, hot feet, lie down, shower, be offered tea and sometimes cake, to sit occasionally in a cold bath to ease aching legs. We met so many B&B owners who had got it right, who really cared. They are a credit to this country.

4. Tears

Oh yes, poor Bob, the tears and the sobs that he had to endure! He must have got fed up at times but never showed it, not for a moment. I particularly remember the last few miles into Wedmore, the descent from Ingleborough, and the arrival at New Lanark, but doubtless Bob could describe many more. I am sure that my tears are one of the defining things for him. Sorry, Bob.

5. Sharing memories

Walking into Bristol, Timperley, Padiham, and home to Kenibus we shared our pasts and our present and our future. We told stories about people we had known, what we had done, and we set out from all those places together, creating more memories that only the two of us can share and understand. They are personal memories of every step, every trial, every joy.

Now it's your turn to walk from Land's End to John O'Groats – and to make your own memories.

Duncansby Stacks, John O'Groats

LIST OF PLACES WE STAYED

Sennen Cove	The Old Success Inn
Gurnard's Head	The Gurnard's Head
Hayle	The White Hart Hotel
Portreath	The Copper House
Perranporth	St George's Country House Hotel
Newquay	Travelodge
Padstow	Simply Padstow
Port Gaverne	Port Gaverne Hotel
Boscastle	The Old Coach House
Widemouth Bay	The Bay View Inn
Bradworthy	Lake House
Great Torrington	Higher Darracott Farm
South Molton	The George Hotel
Withypool	King's Farm
Roadwater	Wood Advent Farm
Radlet	Radlet House
Wedmore	The Swan
Draycott	Oakland House
Rickford	Plume of Feathers
Bristol	Saco Apartments self-catering
Chepstow	Racecourse Guest House
Parkend	Deanfield
Ross-on-Wye	King's Head Hotel
Hereford	The Town House
Leominster	Copper Hall
Pembridge	Lowe Farm
Knighton	Fleece House

Knighton	Cosy Cottage self catering
Three Gates	Newhouse Farm
Forden	The Checkers (Montgomery)
Four Crosses	Rhandregynwen Hall
Rhydycroesau	Pen-y-Dyffryn Hotel
Llangollen	Geifron Hall
Rossett	Rossett Hall
Chester	My niece's house
Cuddington	My sister's house
Knutsford	The Rose and Crown
Salford	Holiday Inn Express
Radcliffe, Ramsbottom, Crawshawbooth, Barley – all stays at our home at Kenibus, near Slaidburn	
Ribblehead	The Station Inn
Outhgill	Ing Hill Lodge
Appleby	Tufton Arms
Langwathby	Fox and Pheasant (Armathwaite)
Park Broom	Park Broom Lodge
Chapel Knowe	Torbeckhill (near Waterbeck)
Moffatt	Bridge House
Abington	Roberton B&B
New Lanark	Scottish Equi B&B
Rosebank	Popinjay Hotel
Glasgow	Grand Central Hotel
Drymen	Ashbank
Rowardennan	Rowardennan Hotel
Inverarnan	Beinglas

Tyndrum	Tyndrum Inn	Alness	Tullochard Guest House
Inveroran	Inveroran Hotel	Tain	Gleed B&B on Morangie Road
Kingshouse	The Kingshouse Hotel	The Mound	2 Quail (Dornoch)
Kinlochleven	Tigh-na-Cheo	Brora	The Royal Marine Hotel
Fort William	The Lime Tree	Ousdale	Navidale House (Navidale)
Gairlochy	The Old Pines	Occumster	Antlers
Invermoriston	Tigh na Bruach	Wick	Clachan
Drumnadrochit	Woodlands Guest House	John O'Groats	Natural Retreats Apartment (self catering)
Inverness	Highland Apartments		
Munlochy	Orcadia		

ACCOMMODATION AND FOOD
The good, the bad and the ugly

We stayed in a huge variety of B&Bs, small hotels and a few self-catering establishments. On the whole, they were all very good and probably much better than would have been the case 10 or 15 years ago. The B&Bs generally outshone the hotels. Great efforts are being made to be excellent, brought about in part by the rise of Trip Advisor and the reviewing system. B&Bs tend to be run by the owners themselves, whereas with hotels this is not always the case and local staff have to be recruited and trained which is not always successful.

The things we appreciated were the following;

- Being able to get an early breakfast, say, 7 or 7.30am

- An immaculately clean warm room

- Tea (& scones or cake!) on arrival

- Radiators or towel rails where we could hand-wash clothes and have them dry and ready the next day

- Plenty of coffee and milk in the room, so that a flask for the following day could be brewed

- A friendly welcome. We were often a trifle dishevelled. Owners and managers who put us at ease always made the stay exceptional. There is nothing worse than feeling as though you're imposing!

Prices varied from £65 per night for both of us including breakfast right up to £150. What's most notable though is that really good accommodation is worth paying for. At 4pm with another two hours to walk, you start praying for a cheery welcome and a good night's sleep and you hope you haven't booked something mean and badly run to save a few pounds.

To be fair, even the accommodation where we thought, "Oh dear!" when we arrived, turned out to have something to recommend it, but the places where they got nearly everything right were a joy to stay in.

Food on the walk is obviously very important but it's the weight, the 'carry-ability' and the endurance that is critical. Food that has gone off, melted, or been crushed won't keep you going, especially if it's got involved with your only clean, dry shirt.

When it comes to eating in the evening, sometimes there's no choice of where to head but on those occasions that the B&B offered a supper, we were always surprised and delighted with what we were served. Breakfasts were nearly always well done, as you might expect. Quite often, if there was a local shop or supermarket, for supper we ate instant soup, cold food and salads in our room.

It's much harder to recommend food to carry with you. If, as above, we ate in our room, we would make a sandwich for the following day, but we almost always carried these staples:

Tin of tuna, butter, crackers, chocolate biscuits, cake, packet soup, tomatoes, salami (keeps well), mints, flask of coffee, sugar, KitKats and, of course, water. With apologies and thanks to Kenneth Grahame. Enjoy!

BEST BITS OF KIT

Most regular walkers have their favourite bits of kit, but here are a few of ours:

Boots
Helen likes very light boots as her feet are 'sensitive'. She went through three pairs of Merrells and still has a couple of pairs of new ones in a cupboard, just in case! I prefer more substantial leather, but again, I didn't complete the walk in the same pair of boots. I did though, 'borrow' a second pair of Zamberlans, already fairly worn in by someone else, for the second half of the walk and they felt like old friends. Maybe even the second hand shops are worth a look for boots already 'run in'. New boots, particularly leather with a solid sole, are always going to give problems to start with so, if you must have a new pair, wear them for strolling around, work or even to bed to get your feet used to them. Some days you have to walk 17 miles and you can't catch a bus if your feet hurt, you just have to walk until the hurting stops!

Waterproofs

Wait until a really wet day comes along and test your waterproofs, and why not your boots? to see if they can really stand up to some serious weather. The jacket has to be comfortable too as it will be worn as much for warmth and to keep the wind off as it will for wet weather. A heavy rucksack with a tight hip belt pulls your waterproofs up, so make sure it's long enough to drop well over your over-trousers. Water doesn't want to be getting in around your middle. The hood on the jacket needs to be good too. When it rains and blows, you need to feel bomb-proof, otherwise your enthusiasm will quickly evaporate, unlike the rain.

Rucksack

If you are buying a new rucksack, take 25lb of stuff with you to put in it when you try it on. When it's on, make sure the hip belt is firmly on your hips, not round your waist or lower than your hips.

Hip belt

That hip belt will save your life, well, your shoulders, neck and back at least. If the rucksack feels heavy, which it will from time to time, tighten the hip belt as often as necessary. Just another notch shifts that weight to the hips and you're walking upright again!

Helen walked with foam sit-mats sandwiched between rucksack strap and shoulders to prevent soreness. She looked ridiculous (her words, not mine!) but the thing is, you don't care. Be comfortable, not stylish.

Other favourite bits of kit include:

Slippers. Really light, comfortable ones you can go to the pub in!

Rucksack cover. Stops the rucksack getting wet and the stuff inside getting damp.

Plastic food boxes. Keeps your travelling food fresh, undamaged and handy. Stock rotation is a must!

Padded sleeveless jackets. Sometimes never even taken out of their bursting Sainsbury's plastic bag, but fabulous to sit on and will warm you up in an instant if you're feeling the cold or in an emergency.

Just two notes: the solar power panels for camping and backpacking which can fit on top of your rucksack are hopeless, at least in this country. You might just charge your phone a fraction with a full day's hot sun on your back. Otherwise, forget it. Save weight by leaving all that solar kit at home, taking a good charger, and, if possible, a spare phone battery.

Mini USB cable devices, on the other hand, are fantastic. I have one cable and plug which does the job for a mini PC (Hannspree), a Bluetooth keyboard (cable is only needed for charging), and for charging a Samsung Camera and Mobile Phone.

FIRST AID

We can't pretend to be qualified first-aiders. You must decide what your first-aid kit should contain and take advice from the myriad of instructional books on walking and long distance backpacking. These are our findings though and we bet you'll use them.

mountainsafety.co.uk recommends	Did we use it?	We also carried
plasters - assorted sizes	barely used	fly repellent (Skin so Soft)
triangular bandage	not taken	tick remover
zinc oxide tape	took insulating tape	Vaseline
disposable gloves	not taken	Savlon
sterile wound dressings	not used	Ibuprofen and Paracetamol
eye bandage	not taken	needle
sterile cleansing wipes	took wet wipes	
tweezers	yes	
scissors	yes	

Helen suffered from Land's End as far as Glasgow with sore feet and blisters. Her practise is to pop blisters if possible, even though it's not always recommended. I don't know how she managed really, but I also don't know why they improved so much after that. I think the fact that from Glasgow we walked the West Highland Way for 10 days with virtually no road-walking helped enormously. Roads and canal towpaths are the places to collect sore feet. The weight of the rucksack is also crucial. Tip over your ideal weight (around 20 lbs for Helen, 26 lbs for me, Bob) and problems will occur. Shin splints were my problem through Devon. A box containing around 9 lb of unnecessary items removed from both our rucksacks was posted home from Great Totterington (Totterington was our joke name, it's actually called Torrington).

Things got much easier after that. Probably the greatest (and cheapest!) solution to aches, pains, sore feet and shin splints was only discovered after a couple of weeks. Cold water! The sea, icy streams and a shower or bath in the evening when you can immerse the painful area in cold water for as long as you can stand it, is an amazing cure. It's no wonder athletes get an ice bath after exercise. Reduce the inflammation as much as possible. Leave a cold flannel on the sore bit. Cover it in Vaseline next day too. Bliss!

NAVIGATION, MAPPING & GPS

Navigation is a pain for some and a delight for others, but you have to know where you are and where you are going at all times. Being lost is to be avoided and could be positively dangerous without the right gear to keep you warm and dry, some emergency provisions and a head-torch with spare batteries, so you can keep going.

We hated taking a wrong path and having to go back over old ground. Even just retracing our steps for a few hundred yards was a major setback, usually leading to swearing at the very least. It's not funny though, if one of you is very tired, to go the wrong way. Strength and determination ebbs quickly away.

Google Maps doesn't yet give you enough detail on the ground, so shouldn't be used for any off road navigation. Ordnance Survey maps are fantastically detailed but heavy and you're often carrying around irrelevant maps for areas just to get the bit you *are* going to cross. The GPS systems in mobile phones are a tremendous boon, but you have to be able to match those co-ordinates to a map and your mobile phone mustn't run out of battery. Carry spare batteries if you can, or something to charge up your phone.

It's possible to print off sections of mapping onto your own A4 sheets, so if you know where your ideal route goes, then print off a 1:25,000 scale section with your route in the middle, so if you veer off you're still likely to be on that map somewhere. It goes without saying you should print on both sides to save weight. We carried around 30 sheets of A4 paper for a couple of week's worth of walking at an average of 15 miles a day. Having that same mapping, or at least the 1:50,000 scale on your mobile phone too means you'll always be able to tell exactly where you are. The 1:25,000 scale mapping shows fences, walls, and even isolated buildings along with some great contour and terrain detail. I know, I know, it's expensive to buy mapping like this, but you need it and needs must.

Your A4 sheets mustn't get wet, so find some way of seeing the map even if it's raining. We used cellophane bags about the size of a greetings card. Ideal.

Whatever you do, enjoy finding a way, sticking to a plan but being prepared to change if one of you gets too tired. On several occasions we caught a bus or train to get to the destination and returned the following morning so we didn't miss a step. Sometimes we did this on a large scale, so we might stay at self-catering accommodation for, say, two nights, using public transport to ferry us back and forth to stay on the walk. Staying at this type of accommodation meant we could usually do some proper washing and cooking, and leave some non essential kit there, so reducing the weight we had to carry for a day or two.

Your chosen route from Land's End to John O'Groats will be yours alone. Nobody else will take exactly the same way and, when you're finished, nobody will be able to take it away from you either.

FOOTPATHS IN THE UK

Ordnance Survey maps show almost 150,000 miles of footpaths in our country. These routes are our inheritance but more importantly, they are trails of our heritage. They are historic pathways which enable us to see what our ancestors got up to, what was important to them, how hard their lives were and how 'on foot' was the only way to travel.

OK, they can get overgrown, but sometimes it is a joy to discover a little-used path, which might take you over a quiet footbridge and connect you with the forgotten past as well as your present objective. I often like to consider what the people who made these tracks were doing or even what they thought about while they used them.

I am sure there are a few discrepancies between what's on the map and what is actually found on the ground, but we found in 99% of cases, the path was exactly where it was marked, and it went exactly as shown on the map. On the whole, footpaths were not blocked or barred. In fields and farmyards, small signs to help you find your way were nearly always in evidence.

Britain's footpaths are also, for the most part, signposted and kept open by local councils - and volunteers in some locations. I salute those people. They made this journey possible and enjoyable by opening up the countryside for anybody to use. You don't pay. They are your 'right' of way. Just get out there, and follow a path - it will eventually get you from Land's End to John O'Groats!

Eglwyseg Cliffs, north of Llangollen

BOB'S ITEMS	Weight gm	Weight oz	HELEN'S ITEMS	Weight gm	Weight oz
Food	2200	77.60	Red Flask full	765	26.98
Flask Full	1450	51.15	Big Socks 2	147	5.19
6 Spare Rechargeable AAAs	76	2.68	Bra 1, Knickers 2	235	8.29
6 Plastic Ties & Blue Tack	18	0.63	Buff, Warm Hat & Cap	158	5.57
2 Bivvy Bags	41	1.45	Fleece	357	12.59
Keyboard & Phone Stand	197	6.95	Glasses 2	74	2.61
Double USB plug	47	1.66	Gloves & Scarf	148	5.22
Compass, Whistle, Headtorch	108	3.81	Gum	111	3.92
2 plastic Knives, Forks, Spoons, Bowls	114	4.02	T Shirt & Skirt	312	11.01
Insulating Tape	53	1.87	Documents, Map Cases	91	3.21
Phone plus all Cables	235	8.29	Headtorch	77	2.72
Spare Phone Battery	33	1.16	Iphone, Plug & Cable	212	7.48
Glasses	23	0.81	Charger & Cables	94	3.32
Gloves & Warm Hat	211	7.44	Paper/notepad/pen	201	7.09
Jumper	311	10.97	Maps, Money & Cards	258	9.10
Sun Hat	35	1.23	Co-codamol & Gaviscon	62	2.19
Slippers	446	15.73	Comb, emery board	20	0.70
Socks & Underpants	95	3.35	Deodorant, Floss, Razor	115	4.06
2 Padded Jackets	897	31.64	Savlon Antiseptic Cream	57	2.01
Plastic Bags, Cup & Food Boxes	243	8.57	Toothpaste & Toothbrush	121	4.27
Rucksack Cover	135	4.76	Washbag, Wet Wipes	150	5.29
Salt & Pepper	55	1.94	Voltarol	43	1.52
Flannel & Nailbrush	85	3.00	Tick Remover	3	0.11
Skin So Soft, Suntan Lotion	91	3.21	Vaseline Lg	60	2.12
Tweezers & Plasters	33	1.16	Sewing Kit & Scissors	39	1.38
Washbag, Toothbrush & Soap, disposable razor	262	9.24	Camera	2580	91.01
Sun Glasses	22	0.78	Sit Mats	42	1.48
Tissues	30	1.06	Railcard, Tickets, Stamps	34	1.20
75cl Water & Bottle	785	27.69	Walking Stick	349	12.31
Sugar & T-Spoon full	469	16.54	Car Key, Whistle	56	1.98
Midge Hats & Shoelaces	78	2.75	Rucksack Cover	94	3.32
Overtrousers & Hi Vis Jacket	248	8.75	Overtrousers	394	13.90
Waterproof Jacket	518	18.27	Waterproof Jacket	719	25.36
Karrimor Rucksack 65 litre	2004	70.69	Rucksack	1746	61.59
Total weight	**12.1 kg**	**26.8 lb**	**Total weight**	**10.1 kg**	**22.3 lb**

Making hay while the sun shines – a good moment to wash and dry Bob's shirt

A DAY OFF – WALKING OR NOT WALKING?

The problem with a day off is you have to join the human race again. It suddenly feels like a race too. Watching the antics of the Appleby folk from a hotel window is almost a treat in itself. From the waking up of a town, to youths shouting obscenities in the dark, the bustle is extraordinary. Why people drive such short distances seems unbelievable. No wonder cities get congested. Even in a small town we're all chasing our tails, parking on double yellow lines and buying bottles of water to keep us hydrated. Water is free! And so are the bottles, once you've bought the first one. Most of the litter by the side of the roads in the UK has been thrown from car windows, and as you walk from Land's End to John O'Groats, you see it. Bottles are, by far, the biggest problem. Why can't we just take the water we need with us every day in our personal water bottle and bring it home at night? OK, rant over.

So you walk all day, then you stop. Stopping suddenly feels scary. It's hard to have a purpose, after days of steadily progressing. Where has the impetus gone? Stop for a cup of tea when you're on a major walk and you feel somehow superior to the locals, who are just killing time after all. You want them all to know your secret. We're walking from Land's End to John O'Groats! Can't you tell?! You want them to know they are in the presence of people who are grasping the nettle, going for gold, pushing back the boundaries!

When you stop walking, you're just normal - or worse, an object of some scorn and amazement because you look terrible, possibly smell a bit sweaty, you don't belong and you obviously have too much time on your hands. That's how people view you all the way, stopped or not. Nearly 60 years old with a big rucksack - it's not natural. Don't start a conversation with them. Weird people to be avoided!

I'm not talking here about just stopping every evening. There's a host of administrative jobs to perform every night which keeps up the momentum of your travel. You wash clothes and try and find somewhere to dry them for the following morning. Feet repairs, rucksack repairs, food to be purchased, maps to be studied, emails to answer.... You have to clean out the flask, clean up yourself... This all forms part of the travelling process.

It's when you stop for a day off, for a month off, or to go home between the different stages of this journey – it's then that you notice a transformation. Your thought processes have changed.

When you are on the walk, the business of onward progression fills every moment of your day and evening. There isn't room in your head for anything else. When you stop the walk, the antonyms for progression are all these words from Thesaurus: 'halt, decrease, impediment, stagnation, hindrance, decline, block, failure, worsening'. Is it more fun to go forward or stay still? Say no more.

THE CAMERA

I carried a Canon EOS 5D Mark III together with a Canon EF f/2.8L IS 70-200mm lens, total weight 5lbs. That doesn't sound a lot. I know some photographers who use medium format or larger pro cameras than the 5D and carry something in the order of 2 stones in weight. But I am not, nor ever will be, one of those photographers who carry masses of equipment, lenses, tripods, filters and so on. I don't do it in my ordinary life as a professional photographer and on this walk, believe me, carrying a non-essential 5lbs-worth of camera for 1,140 miles was quite enough. Many people said to me: why not take just a small bridge camera and keep the weight down? But there was no way on earth I was walking the length of my country without my wonderful 5D! In an ideal world I would have also carried my wide angle lens to capture some of the amazing vistas we came across, but on balance I decided that extra bit of weight wasn't justified. Wide angles were taken with my iphone instead.

I don't have the patience to sit and wait for a shot, and on this walk there was no waiting to be had anyway. If the shot was there when we walked past, I tried to capture it. It was as simple as that. I know I missed some great shots because there wasn't time to get the camera out of the rucksack, but it was too uncomfortable to carry it on my shoulder or in my hand all the time, so Bob acted as 'head grip' and he retrieved the camera from my rucksack whilst still on my back, then put it back and fastened me up again. Occasionally he carried the camera for me and the roles were reversed and I can tell you, 1,140 miles of acting as key grip must not have been a whole lot of fun for him. I am immensely grateful that he tolerated it.

POSTSCRIPT

You're doing the dishes, driving to work, walking round the shops or something else fairly mundane and then suddenly, wham! one of the hundreds of places and memories from the walk flashes back right in front of your eyes. You recall what it looked like, how you felt and how it smelt, what the weather was doing. You remember the freedom, the elation, the struggle, the journey. What a fantastic thing you did and how you wish you were doing it again! Like a stick of rock, you have 'Land's End to John O'Groats' running right through your core. You are full of happy memories.

Years from now, it'll be your point of reference. When you travel up or down the country and you cross your 'route', you'll say to yourself, 'Wow, I walked to this point from Land's End. Been here, done that. Best thing I ever did.'

You'll become an expert on the geography of Great Britain. When someone asks politely, 'Have you done much walking?', you'll gently drop it into the conversation and wait for the intake of breath.

Walking from Land's End to John O'Groats is the ultimate travel adventure: it is epic, heroic marching, covering hard ways, many ancient ways and now you have made them your ways.

You pass some deer in a wood, the alpha male eying you up. It is poised to turn away, but for that moment its look is telling you, 'This is my wood, these are my tracks and pathways.' Almost arrogant, mightily sure of itself, it

seems to be saying, 'This time I'll let you pass this way and then you will be gone, but remember: I'll always be here, stealthy and hidden, quiet and powerful, serene and beautiful.'

And eventually that's how you'll feel. You've walked past everyone's back garden. Quietly and unobtrusively. Respectfully and with purpose. Most people didn't even know you were there and if they did spot you, you gave them the same stare as the deer.

'I'm here and this is my place. These are my ways. As a human being, this land is mine and I love every inch of it. I know where I am, who I am, and where I'm going'. All the way from Land's End to John O'Groats.

JOHN O' GROATS

A Welcome at the End of the Road

The End!